How to End the 'Monetarist' Controversy

A Journalist's Reflections on Output, Jobs, Prices and Money

SAMUEL BRITTAN

Published by

THE INSTITUTE OF ECONOMIC AFFAIRS

1981

First published in July 1981

© THE INSTITUTE OF ECONOMIC AFFAIRS 1981

ISSN 0073-2818
ISBN 0-255 36144-0

Printed in England by

GORON PRO-PRINT CO LTD
6 Marlborough Road, Churchill Industrial Estate, Lancing, W. Sussex

Text set in 'Monotype' Baskerville

CONTENTS

*[The use of asterisks in the text is explained on page 14.—ED.]

[4]

[5]

PREFACE

The *Hobart Papers* are intended to contribute a stream of authoritative, independent and lucid analyses to the understanding and application of economics to private and government activity. The characteristic theme has been the optimum use of scarce resources and the extent to which it can best be achieved in markets within an appropriate framework of law and institutions or, where markets cannot work, in other ways. Since in the real world the alternative to the market is the state, and both are imperfect, the choice between them effectively turns on judgement of the comparative consequences of 'market failure' and 'government failure'.

The management of the monetary system to oil the wheels of the economy was long regarded by economists as one of the indispensable functions of government in creating the framework of law and institutions. Monetary management was promoted to an even more urgent task when, after the Great Depression of 1929-32, unemployment, described earlier by William Beveridge as 'a problem of *industry*', was made a problem of *government* by J. M. Keynes. Monetary management, or specifically the management of demand for goods and services and therefore labour, was thus made a dominant subject of economic science and a prevailing policy of government in the post-war Western world. Since the late 1960s the theoretical foundation for the proposition that demand management could remove unemployment without uncontrollable inflation has been increasingly challenged by economists who emphasised the control of the quantity of money in the mastery of inflation. In the last two years the challengers have themselves been questioned by economists who held to the Keynesian approach and who have claimed that control of the money supplied since 1979 has in turn failed to master inflation except at a prohibitive cost in unemployment.

In Hobart Paper 90 Mr Samuel Brittan re-examines the essence of the 'counter-revolution' against Keynes in a wide-ranging review of the theoretical debate. His central purpose is to clarify the issues by showing the light that can be thrown on them by the two main schools of thought in their varying forms. By removing misunderstandings and sifting the wheat from the chaff, he will help a wide range of readers, from student newcomers to economics to practitioners of economic processes in industry and policies in government, to understand the disputations and debates among economists that continue to dominate the formation of public policy whatever the political colour of government.

Although he styles himself a journalist, Mr Brittan's writings in refining economic thought and its applications reveal him as a foremost economic scholar. And in clarifying economic concepts and controversies he shows himself also as a teacher of an abstract social science that explains much of daily life in households, industry and government.

Although the constitution of the Institute requires it to dissociate its Trustees, Directors and Advisers from the arguments and conclusions of its authors, it presents Mr Brittan's *Hobart Paper* as a scholarly, authoritative and thought-provoking *tour d'horizon* of the economics of inflation and unemployment that will help to focus attention on the essentials. In so doing it suggests the grounds for a wide measure of agreement among economists and politicians who desire that the effective solutions shall not be interminably deferred by avoidable misunderstanding.

May 1981   ARTHUR SELDON

QUOTATIONS FROM THE AUTHOR'S
PREVIOUS WORKS

'Both fiscal and monetary policy are means of managing demand and controlling the flow of money expenditure. The basic questions raised by the works of Friedman and the monetarists associated with him turn on (a) whether it would be better to place less reliance on discretionary short-term policy and more on long-term guidelines in both the fiscal and the monetary field, and (b) the contention that demand management by whatever means cannot by itself achieve a predetermined target rate of unemployment or any other real variable.'

(Capitalism and the Permissive Society,
Macmillan, 1973, p. 179.)

'Whether demand is best regulated by monetary or fiscal policy is a subordinate, technical question in this context. In the narrow sense the issue of "monetarism" is one which politicians and commentators are wise to leave to experts . . . The argument of the critics of post-war orthodoxy is ultimately about the nature of labour markets and the limitations of conventional full employment policies.'

(Second Thoughts on Full Employment Policy,
Barry Rose for the Centre for Policy Studies, 1975,
pp. 15-17.)

THE AUTHOR

SAMUEL BRITTAN was born in 1933 and educated at Kilburn Grammar School and Jesus College, Cambridge, where he took First-Class Honours in economics. He then held various posts on the *Financial Times* (1955-61); was Economics Editor of the *Observer* (1961-64); an Adviser at the Department of Economic Affairs (1965); and has been principal economic commentator on the *Financial Times* since 1966.

He was the first winner of the Senior Wincott Award for financial journalism in 1971. He was a Research Fellow of Nuffield College in 1973-74 and in 1974 was elected a Visiting Fellow. In 1978 he was a Visiting Professor at the Chicago Law School.

His publications include *Steering the Economy* (third edition, Penguin, 1971); *Left or Right: The Bogus Dilemma* (Secker & Warburg, 1968); *The Price of Economic Freedom: A Guide to Flexible Rates* (Macmillan, 1970); *Is There An Economic Consensus?* (Macmillan, 1973); *Capitalism and the Permissive Society* (Macmillan, 1973); (with Peter Lilley) *The Delusion of Incomes Policy* (Maurice Temple Smith, 1977); *The Economic Consequences of Democracy* (Maurice Temple Smith, 1977). For the IEA he has written *Government and the Market Economy* (Hobart Paperback No. 2, 1971), and *Participation without Politics* (Hobart Paper No. 62, 1975, 2nd Edn., 1979).

ACKNOWLEDGEMENTS

I am indebted to Dr Alan Budd of the London Business School who read the manuscript at very short notice, and made many helpful suggestions. Thanks are also due to Arthur Seldon and Martin Wassell for their editorial help and encouragement.

S.B.

This above all: to thine own self be true,
And it must follow, as the night the day,
Thou canst not then be false to any man.

(*Hamlet*, Act 1, Scene 3)

The letter killeth, but the spirit giveth life.

(The Second Epistle of St. Paul to the Corinthians)

I. INTRODUCTION

This *Hobart Paper* arises out of a sense of frustration with the
way in which economic policy is commonly discussed. The
forces affecting output, jobs, prices and money in the aggregate
are the traditional subject-matter of what is known as macro-
economics.

Unfortunately, public discussion of these questions has been
bedevilled by the political symbolism acquired by that accursed
word 'monetarism' and by the professional difficulty economists (like all other specialists) experience in distinguishing the
wood from the trees. The campaign of vilification has been so
successful that many educated citizens believe the principal
tenet of 'monetarism' to be support for Latin American dic-
tatorships employing torture. Those of a more charitable dis-
position suppose it to be a label for hardships deliberately
imposed on peoples by governments to punish them for laziness
or poor productivity.

Even if we ignore political polemics and concentrate on the
narrow economic debate, we come across a minefield of terms
which are either ambiguous or do not mean what they seem to
mean. Not only 'monetarism' but many other expressions such
as 'incomes policy', 'natural rate of unemployment', 'deflation',
'growth', and 'demand management' come into this category.

Nor has understanding been helped by official explanations
of economic policy. Questions of broad principle, about which
every interested citizen has a right to be informed, have been
hopelessly mixed up with highly technical questions of strictly

[11]

specialist interest. A lot has been said by both Labour and Conservative administrations in Britain, by the US Federal Reserve, and by heads of government at summit meetings, about the need to limit public sector borrowing and monetary expansion. But very little has been said to explain why these limitations are necessary. At times it has even looked as if the choice of a particular wing of a particular political party to support has depended on the quirks of monthly figures understood only by a handful of experts in banking theory, if by them.

This is, of course, absurd. The key issues do not lie in banking technicalities. The subject crying out for explanation is the counter-revolution[1] which has dethroned post-war full employment policies. Until the late 1960s, '500,000 unemployed' was a crisis level in the UK leading to policy reversals and the sacking of Cabinet Ministers. In the early 1970s, the alarm bells rang at 1 million; in the late 1970s, at $1\frac{1}{2}$ million. In the early 1980s, the burning question is whether unemployment can be held below the 3 million mark.

The 1981 Budget aimed, rightly or wrongly, to increase tax revenue by £4 billion (compared with what would have been raised if thresholds and specific duties had been adjusted for inflation but no other changes made). Yet traditional post-war criteria would have suggested a need to do just the opposite and inject into the British economy spending power of at least £20 billion that year: say, to reduce taxes by £10 billion and raise government spending by the same amount. Nothing remotely like this was on the cards, either through policy changes by the Government in office or through the actions of any likely successors.

No economic school has explained satisfactorily the steep trend rise in unemployment. The counter-revolutionaries can explain something more modest—an explanation given *long before the event* of why post-war attempts by governments to spend their way into target levels of employment would eventually fail, and why therefore such policies would be useless for dealing with present problems.

---

[1] The origin in my mind of the term 'counter-revolution' is Milton Friedman's Wincott Memorial Lecture, *The Counter-Revolution in Monetary Theory*, Occasional Paper 33, IEA, 1970, and Harry Johnson's riposte, 'The Keynesian Revolution and the Monetarist Counter-Revolution', reprinted in *On Economics and Society*, University of Chicago Press, Chicago, 1975.

An observer's view of the counter-revolution

The main object of this *Paper* is to present one observer's view of the counter-revolution. It will then be possible to place the narrower arguments about money in better perspective. A counter-revolution is not the same as mere reaction. A genuine counter-revolution should absorb the best elements of the revolution it is replacing; or, to change the metaphor, should keep the baby while emptying out the bathwater. This *Paper* attempts to apply this injunction to the ideas of 'demand management' associated with Lord Keynes.

My own view is that the most important and valuable doctrines of Keynes are almost identical with the most important and valuable doctrines of Friedman. This *Paper* seeks to highlight this identity in terms of a simple objective of policy which will enable governments to achieve what can be achieved by central financial policy to prevent avoidable unemployment and depression as well as runaway inflation.

For the sake of clarity and familiarity most of the data in the early sections are taken from the UK. But they are used to illustrate problems which affect most countries and the international economy as a whole. No attempt is made to focus on the particular parochial problems which are most topical at the time of writing. My main policy proposal will provide some re-assurance to those who fear that a high sterling exchange rate will lead to massive depression—if it is still an issue when they come to read it. But the approach will be indirect and not *via* an exchange-rate target. The quickest way to the other side of a hill is not always to climb over the top.

The economics of politics—and economics?

A new branch of economics labelled 'public choice theory' or the 'economics of politics' has come into existence, which the IEA has done much to promulgate on this side of the Atlantic.[1] It treats politicians and civil servants not as platonic guardians of the public welfare but as people trying to serve their own interest in the political market-place, just as businessmen and workers do in the commercial market-place.

A still newer, if minor, branch is now needed called the 'economics of economics'. Such a study would start from the

[1] J. M. Buchanan *et al.*, *The Economics of Politics*, IEA Readings 18, IEA, 1978; Gordon Tullock, *The Vote Motive*, Hobart Paperback 9, 1976; William A. Niskanen, *Bureaucracy: Servant or Master?*, Hobart Paperback 5, 1973.

recognition that academic economics is itself an industry in which people compete for chairs, foundation money and other benefits, and not simply a disinterested search for knowledge. This *Paper* is not meant as a contribution to that industry. It concentrates on what appears to me the key or interesting issues and passes very quickly over some of the main current preoccupations of textbooks and academic papers.

Even so, some abstraction and some degree of detail have been difficult to avoid. Naturally, readers will have differing preoccupations. I have marked with an asterisk those passages which are not essential for readers who want to grasp the broad drift of the argument as quickly as possible.

Nothing gave me more trouble in writing this *Paper* than arriving at the appropriate order. Section III, 'The Supply Response', analyses how output, prices and employment respond to demand stimuli. It should logically have come first since it is the key to the whole argument. But it is much the most difficult, if only because I have not found a way to simplify the issues to my own satisfaction. I have, therefore, begun with a Section II, 'Demand Management Re-appraised', which can be read on its own. Some readers may want to move from there straight to Section VI, 'Jobs and Pay', the importance of which needs no underlining, before tackling the intermediate Sections. The Appendix to that Section on the 'lump of labour fallacy' is much the most important part of this *Paper*.

*   *   *

The larger part of this *Paper* was completed before the much-heralded 1981 Report of the House of Commons Treasury and Civil Service Committee on Monetary Policy.[1] But, as I feared, that Report served mainly to underline the need for an exposition which attempts to distinguish the wood from the trees. The famous 'Statement of Economic Policy' of '364 university economists' calling for a rejection of 'monetarist policies' served to emphasise further the need to explain the fundamentals of the counter-revolution in economic thinking with which so many who pronounce on policy have still to come to terms.

---

[1] Third Report from the House of Commons Treasury and Civil Service Committee, Session 1980-81: *Monetary Policy*, Vol. I: *Report*, HC 163-I, HMSO, 1981.

II. DEMAND MANAGEMENT RE-APPRAISED

The narrow counter-revolution

During the late 1960s, more attention began to be paid to monetary matters by policy-makers in both the USA and Britain. Until then demand management had been seen in both countries largely in terms of fiscal policy. A minority of economists had always thought this a mistaken emphasis. They maintained that neglect of monetary policy was a grave error. They also believed that to assess monetary policy it was necessary to look directly at measures of money and credit, since interest rates gave a misleading indication. High nominal interest rates could mean low or even negative real ones in a period of inflation. Real interest rates are, however, extremely difficult to calculate since the discount for expected inflation is a highly subjective matter. Even if this obstacle could be surmounted, it was doubtful if central banks had the knowledge to calculate the real interest rate appropriate at any particular time.

These contentions achieved headline status as a result of two events. In the USA a tax increase, won from Congress by President Johnson to offset the inflationary forces set off by the Vietnam War, took effect in 1968, and there was a large swing out of deficit in the Federal Budget. The fiscal tightening failed to have its expected restraining effect until the Federal Reserve Board responded by reducing sharply the rate of monetary expansion at the end of the year.

The second event was in the UK when, despite a highly restrictive fiscal policy, the 1967 devaluation proved slow to work and domestic consumption rose more than forecast. Partly on IMF insistence, monetary policy was tightened and the Government adopted for 1969-70 a ceiling of £400 million on Domestic Credit Expansion (DCE)—which can be regarded as the domestic component of monetary growth. Indeed, the last year and a half of the Chancellorship of Mr Roy Jenkins witnessed the firmest conscious control of the quantity of money of any period in British post-war history. The quantity of money in the UK was allowed to go through the roof again under the Heath Government of the early 1970s;

[15]

but preoccupation with monetary magnitudes came back, first under Mr Denis Healey who became Labour Chancellor in 1974, and then under the Thatcher Government which took office in 1979.

Seen as a shift of emphasis from fiscal to monetary policy, the challenge to post-war orthodoxy was purely in the realm of technical means. Monetarism as a technical doctrine was often summed up in the slogan 'There is a stable demand function for money'. This phrase meant that the amount of money people wished to hold was closely related in a predictable way to the national income in money terms; and that, if there was more money, national income would rise correspondingly. This proposition was underpinned by a second one—more often implied than explicitly asserted: that there was a sharp break between money and other assets. Otherwise the restriction of whatever was defined as money could be circumvented by an expansion of money substitutes. The two propositions were often supposed to imply the third proposition already mentioned: that monetary rather than fiscal policy determined aggregate demand and national income; and that fiscal policy, whatever its importance for other purposes, was largely irrelevant to demand management.

In practice, the original technical controversy about whether monetary or fiscal policy matters most is as dead as the dodo on this side of the Atlantic and only just flickering in the United States. American economists who call themselves Keynesians would now be the first to emphasise that monetary policy affects demand and that it must be correctly tied in with fiscal policy. On the Continent of Europe, fiscal policy never enjoyed quite the rôle it was assigned in its heyday in Britain; and monetary policy was never so downgraded. Even in Britain it is extremely unlikely that any government bent on pursuing either an expansionary or contractionary demand policy would today examine only the fiscal indicators and ignore the monetary ones.

On the other side of the fence, British economists who are labelled 'monetarists' are the first to emphasise that a major long-run influence on the quantity of money is the Public Sector Borrowing Requirement (PSBR) which is, of course, a measure of fiscal policy; and some even stress that a high PSBR can have an influence on demand and prices in its own right. They argue that if interest rates are raised by heavy

[16]

government borrowing, people will want to hold smaller money balances. A given quantity of money will thus support a higher nominal GDP and velocity will increase. Unlike Friedman, they argue that this is an important effect.[1]

Arguments about these propositions, however exciting or provocative to national income forecasters or monetary specialists, are not issues to split politicians into warring camps and cause families and friends to part company. Yet the passions set off by the word 'monetarism' have intensified rather than abated since the late 1960s. Voters do not choose between parties on the basis of conflicting views of the income *versus* the interest elasticity of demand for money. Cabinets are not formed on the basis of views about the degree of substitutability between bank advances, bank bills and inter-company credits. Behind all the smoke there must be some fire of a different kind. Let us start again.

Monetary and fiscal policy are both simply means of influencing total spending—or, in more technical language, 'aggregate demand'. What exactly does this expression mean? It is so much at the centre of analysis, forecasting and policy that it cannot be avoided. But it is not the happiest of expressions. The demand for one commodity, say, apples of a certain kind in a specific area over a specific time, has a reasonably clear meaning. It is either the quantity of apples that can be sold at a given price, or the whole relationship ('demand curve') expressing the volume and value of sales that would be possible at different prices. Things become much more complicated when we think of the whole economy. If a producer raises or lowers his prices, his action will have ripple effects through other markets which will react on his own conditions.

Nevertheless, most businessmen can give a rough common-sense meaning to the 'general state of demand'. If the value or volume of goods which can be profitably sold has fallen, not in one line of business but across the board, it makes sense to talk of 'depressed demand'. Of course, all that can be measured

---

[1] One estimate suggests that a 1 per cent increase in the stock of government debt held outside the banks leads eventually to a rise in the price level of just under 0·4 per cent. A 1 per cent increase in the money stock on its own produces a rise in the price level of just over 0·6 per cent. A 1 per cent increase in both money and outstanding bonds leads to a rise in the price level of about 1 per cent. (Michael Beenstock, 'The Debate About Monetary Ceilings', *Economic Outlook, 1980-1984*, London Business School, Gower Publishing, Vol. 5, No. 1, October 1980.)

is total spending at actual prices—not hypothetical levels which would prevail if prices were different. In an analysis of the movement of national income statistics 'aggregate demand' has to be identified with the total flow of spending or, for those who prefer to be more polysyllabic, 'aggregate expenditure'.

*Aggregate demand—what does it mean?**

Since almost everything that follows hangs on this idea, it is essential to be extremely clear what it means. Total spending is in practice measured by the 'Gross Domestic Product at Current Market Prices', often called for short 'Money GDP' or, in American parlance, 'Nominal GDP'.

Money GDP can be conceived in two ways. It is the product of the quantity of money multiplied by its velocity of circulation in current transactions; or, in symbols, MV: money times velocity (of circulation). It can also be broken down into 'Real GDP', i.e. the GDP expressed at the prices prevailing in some particular year, multiplied by a price index. This is the right-hand side of the famous equation $MV=PT$. The term 'T' refers only to transactions generating *new* net output or value added. The sale of old houses, second-hand cars, shares or other existing assets has to be excluded, as well as intermediate transactions, if we are to apply it to the national income figures published by government statistical offices throughout the world.

There are many other synonyms (listed in Table I) in use for 'total spending' or 'Money GDP' or MV. One reason for this proliferation is that, in national income accounting, the circular flow of spending can be measured as expenditure, output or income. The three methods ought in principle to yield the same figures, although in practice there are bound to be discrepancies in measurement.

Another, linguistic, source of multiplicity of labels is the American habit of using 'nominal' where British writers prefer 'monetary', or 'money' in its adjectival sense. Thus 'monetary demand', 'total expenditure', 'GDP at current market prices', 'nominal GDP', and 'nominal national income' mean much the same thing. They measure the total flow of money spending either at the point of expenditure, or when it emerges as output, or when it is paid out in income.

'Total spending' is probably the best term for popular presentation and 'Money GDP' for reporting economic statis-

TABLE I

GDP AT CURRENT MARKET PRICES:
INCOMPLETE LIST OF NEAR SYNONYMS

UK usage	*US usage*
Money GDP	Nominal GDP
Total Demand ⎱ at current prices	
Aggregate Demand ⎰	
Monetary Demand	Nominal Demand
MV (Money times velocity)	
Total Spending	Nominal Spending
Aggregate Expenditure at current prices	Nominal Expenditure
Money National Product	Nominal National Product
Money Value of National Output	Nominal Output
Money National Income	Nominal National Income
	Total Nominal Income
Total Incomes	Nominal Income

tics. 'Total incomes' can also be used in discussion, but risks giving the impression that the speaker is talking about what the public knows as 'incomes policy' when he is really referring to demand management.

Control of total spending

The main advantage of talking in terms of total spending or Money GDP is that the precise definition of 'money' becomes a secondary issue. We can say that the average outstanding stock of money, measured by sterling M3, was £55 billion in 1979 and velocity was 3·5. We can alternatively take the narrower 'M1' definition of money, which excludes deposit (in US parlance 'savings') accounts, and say that this amounted to about £28 billion and that velocity was about 6·8. Either way we arrive back at a Money GDP of around £190 billion.

Some people have misunderstood this suggestion by responding: 'It is difficult enough to control money; do you want to regulate velocity as well?' The last thing we need are separate targets for M and for V. The government and the central bank are all the time influencing total spending (MV) by the size of public sector deficits and the way they are financed, by changing interest rates or the ability of banks to lend, and sometimes too by exchange rate intervention and direct credit controls. My suggestion is that these operations should have as their ultimate target Money GDP, i.e. MV considered jointly as a flow.

This can be illustrated by the experience of 1980 when the growth of the quantity of money measured by sterling M3 accelerated alarmingly in the course of the year to twice the official target rate. Yet price inflation slowed down and output dropped. By analysing MV together we can avoid getting bogged down in the semantic question of whether velocity fell or whether the official figures exaggerated the true growth of the quantity of money. Of course, these technical questions matter for the implementation of policy, but they are subordinate to the bigger question of whether the growth of MV decelerated too much or too little or by the right amount in 1980. If objectives here are unclear, we will not be sure about our desired destination however much we improve our navigational techniques.

If Keynesian teaching is about the need to manage or at least to watch monetary or nominal demand, then we all ought to be Keynesians. The reason why demand management has been discredited is that policy-makers in the post-war period switched the focus from *nominal* to *real* demand—or, in terms of the published figures, from 'Money GDP' to 'GDP at constant prices'. The reader has only to consult a typical economic forecast to see that most magnitudes are valued at constant (usually 1975) prices.

This shift to 'real demand' was a fatal error. For it begged the question of how far a boost to spending raised output and how far it was dissipated in an inflationary increase of prices and wages.[1] In the heyday of 'real demand' management, governments and their advisers had a target of, say, 1¾ to 2 per cent unemployment, equivalent to less than 450,000 people. If unemployment was forecast to rise above that target,

---

[1] It would be pleasant to exculpate Keynes himself from this misjudgement; but I am afraid that he encouraged bad habits by writing much of the *General Theory* in terms of a particular kind of funny money known as 'wage units'. But not all Keynesians have followed this bad habit. In the US in particular the Council of Economic Advisers has quite often examined past and prospective changes in *nominal* national product before estimating the breakdown between changes in price and changes in quantity.

demand was supposed to be boosted by tax cuts, higher spending, credit relaxations, and so on. That such boosts tended to take a budgetary form, with the money supply responding passively, was a secondary matter. The same underlying philosophy could just as well have been allied with planned changes in the money supply if that had been thought the appropriate weapon. The belief was that a sufficient boost to demand would raise output and reduce unemployment until the target was reached. If unemployment threatened to fall too low ('overfull employment'), the government would restrain demand; but it usually required a sterling crisis before it would restrain demand in a major way.

There were many arguments about whether the government should aim at a pressure of demand corresponding to $1\frac{1}{2}$, $1\frac{3}{4}$ or $2\frac{1}{4}$ per cent unemployment, and there was nearly as much mudslinging over that question as over 'monetarism' today. Professor Frank Paish suffered torrents of abuse for preferring the $2\frac{1}{4}$ per cent figure[1] which Ministers today would give their eye-teeth to achieve.

Despite the official doctrines, governments did not always boost demand when unemployment rose above the chosen target; and they sometimes took restrictive measures even when recession loomed and unemployment was expected to rise. The alibi was invariably the threat of an overseas payments deficit or a run on the pound. Thus it came to look as if the fixed exchange rate for sterling was the main constraint on the growth of output. It was rarely suggested, even by the 'sound money men' of the time, that there were any obstacles, apart from the balance of payments, to achieving chosen output and employment levels. Together, the main industrial countries in pre-OPEC days were in current payments balance or surplus. Thus it seemed according to this philosophy that, if they expanded together, they could spend themselves into chosen levels of economic activity.

It hardly ever occurred to the exponents of the dominant orthodoxy that the main effect of boosting demand might be on prices rather than output. Inflation was usually regarded as due to wage push, emanating more or less from outside the economic system, or just occasionally from import prices over which an industrial country had little control. The way to

[1] F. W. Paish, *Rise and Fall of Incomes Policy*, Hobart Paper 47, IEA, 1969 (2nd Edition 1971).

limit inflation, it was assumed, was to control wages by statute; or, if this was politically inexpedient, by deals with, or exhortation to, trade union leaders.[1]

The past tense has been used because no major Western economy is run in this way at the moment. But many politicians, officials, and economists still see demand management, employment and prices in these terms.[2] They see various 'hideous obstacles' to traditional demand management ranging from OPEC and oil shortages to financial markets ignorantly obsessed with public sector borrowing requirements and monetary figures. These factors are treated as chance misfortunes; and if only they could be circumvented we could, it is supposed, go back to demand management in real terms aimed at chosen levels of output and employment.

'Nominal' versus 'real'

A little reflection (always easier after the event) should have shown that all governments and central bankers can regulate directly by demand management consists of flows of money. (In other words, control is over the left-hand, or MV, side of the identity on page 18.) The error of most post-war demand management was to assume that real things, such as output and employment, could invariably and as a matter of course be affected permanently by financial manipulation.

Governments were slow to realise this limitation of their powers. When accustomed injections of monetary demand no longer yielded the expected result in output and employment, but were largely dissipated in inflation, the dose was stepped up. This is a common experience among drug addicts who need stronger and stronger doses to regain the old 'kicks'. But, in contrast to drug addicts, governments did not always realise what they were doing. They thought they were stimulating or at least bolstering output and employment, when they were in practice boosting Money GDP, with the main effects on the price component.

[1] S. Brittan, *Steering the Economy*, Penguin Books, 1971.

[2] The *locus classicus* of the orthodox post-war British attitude to demand management can be found in the Ninth Report from the House of Commons Expenditure Committee, *Public Expenditure, Inflation and the Balance of Payments*, 1974, especially in the evidence of official witnesses, e.g. Lord Kahn and Dr Michael Posner. A notable exponent of this outlook at the time of writing is Mr Peter Shore, Labour Shadow Chancellor.

The dissipation in rising prices of past demand increases is shown clearly in Chart 1. During the first quinquennium, 1959-64, nominal demand, as measured by Money GDP, grew by nearly 38 per cent; slightly over half of the growth was reflected in increased output and slightly less than half in higher prices. The expansion of nominal demand was stepped up in successive periods, but more and more of the growth was reflected in inflation and less and less in higher output. By the time of the last recorded period, 1974-79, the rise in nominal demand of nearly 130 per cent was reflected almost entirely in higher prices, while output growth was less than half its rate during the first quinquennium.

The figures in the Chart are neither a tautology nor a statement of the obvious, as hasty critics suggest. As a matter of arithmetic, successively larger demand boosts *could* have been reflected in a faster rise in output. But they *were* reflected in more rapid inflation and slower real growth than ever before. The events occurred partly because of the puncturing of 'money illusion' (discussed below) and partly because underlying *non-monetary* forces were pulling down growth rates and pushing up unemployment. These forces were misinterpreted as demand deficiency, and nominal expenditure was encouraged to gallop ahead in a vain attempt to regain previous growth and employment rates.

The treatment of shocks

There is still, however, a question about the exact rôle of governments and central banks in periods of rapidly rising money GDP, of the kind shown in the Chart. Have they initiated these rapid rises—whether from a mistaken desire to 'stimulate' the economy, from electorally-motivated increases in public spending, or for any other reason? Or have they mainly accommodated inflationary impulses originating elsewhere?

The general price level does not suddenly leap upwards of its own accord. A price or cost push is possible because individual prices or wages are slower to adjust themselves to downward than to upward pressure. This is often called 'downward wage and price rigidity', but sluggishness or resistance is a more accurate description. It therefore follows that sudden and unexpected rises in some major costs or prices will provide a shock to the system. The failure of other prices to fall straightaway in

CHART 1

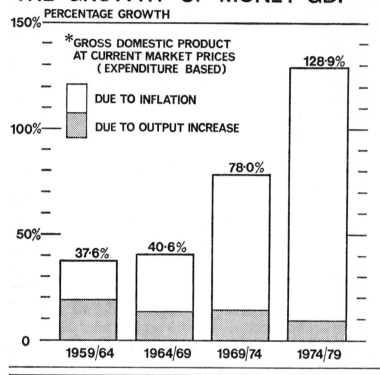

THE GROWTH OF MONEY GDP*

PERCENTAGE GROWTH

*GROSS DOMESTIC PRODUCT
AT CURRENT MARKET PRICES
(EXPENDITURE BASED)

☐ DUE TO INFLATION

▨ DUE TO OUTPUT INCREASE

| | 1959/64 | 1964/69 | 1969/74 | 1974/79 |
| | 37·6% | 40·6% | 78·0% | 128·9% |

GDP AT MARKET PRICES (EXPENDITURE BASED)

PERCENTAGE CHANGE OVER PERIOD

PERIOD	TOTAL INCREASE at current prices	OUTPUT INCREASE at 1975 prices	** INCREASE IN PRICES
1959/64	+ 37·6	+ 19·4	+ 15·2
1964/69	+ 40·6	+ 13·2	+ 24·2
1969/74	+ 78·0	+ 14·1	+ 56·0
1974/79	+ 128·9	+ 9·3	+ 109·4

** MEASURED BY GROSS DOMESTIC EXPENDITURE DEFLATOR

compensation will lead to an initial rise in the overall price level (P) and to a decline in activity and employment (T) if the government stands firm in its control of MV.

Sometimes the initiating force comes from the 'MV', or demand, side in which government is usually predominant, and sometimes from the 'PT', or supply, side. In the latter case government still plays an essential but passive rôle in allowing the expansion to occur. The second oil price rise of 1978-80 was probably a genuine supply shock. The indices of world monetary growth and of budget deficits showed little or no prior acceleration. The shock came from the oil market when the dollar price of crude rose by 150 per cent. On the other hand, the oil price explosion of 1973-74, although triggered off by the Arab-Israeli War, was in large part a response to excessive and synchronised demand expansion in the major industrialised economies, which also showed itself in a doubling of non-oil commodity prices.

Union wage push

Union wage push is best understood as one example of a supply shock. An existing degree of union monopoly power or strike-threat power affects the distribution of *relative* wages between occupations and industries. Wages will be higher and employment lower in the more effectively unionised sectors than they would be in a competitive market, while wages will be lower and employment higher in the less effectively unionised or non-unionised sectors. But there is nothing here to start off a new inflationary trend or aggravate an existing one.

Suppose, however, that a major group of unions increases its degree of monopoly power or makes more use of its existing power. This can be the result of a thousand and one factors. For instance, there may be increased organisation or membership, or more militant tactics. Such changes may be a reaction to a period of government wage control. They can stem from pressure on real take-home pay due to a worsening of the nation's terms of trade. They can be due to legislation, such as that of 1974-76, deliberately designed to increase union power. Nor is there any reason to rule out changing political currents or key personalities.

Whatever the initiating force, the result is the same as with other shocks. As wages and prices outside the union sector are most unlikely to fall immediately to anything like an offsetting

[25]

extent, prices will rise even if MV remains stable, and activity and employment will fall, i.e. P will rise at the expense of T.

How far should monetary demand be adjusted upwards to accommodate supply shocks whose initial effect is to raise the price level? At one extreme there is a policy of non-accommodation. The target growth for MV is maintained, and an output slump accepted, until the agents in the economy—employees and employers, savers and investors—realise what is happening and some prices and wages fall (or rise less quickly than before) by a sufficient amount to offset the rise in those directly affected by the shock.

Next along the scale comes a policy of *minimal accommodation*. In other words, there is a once-for-all rise in monetary demand, MV, to accommodate, for instance, the direct impact of an OPEC price rise. But there is no further accommodation for secondary wage claims stimulated by the oil-induced rise in the cost of living. The increase in MV is thus once-for-all. It is made clear that the abnormally large rise in the price level in the period of shock will not be allowed to trigger a lasting increase in the rate of inflation.

Beyond this there are any number of degrees of accommodation (or 'permissiveness') in demand management. Secondary wage increases triggered off by the shock rise in the general price level may be accommodated, but for one year only. Some people would want to go further and accept the increase in inflationary expectations as a fact of life and permanently raise the target path for MV. But what then happens if there are further adverse shocks, as there are very likely to be? Each successive shock and each successive piece of accommodation will jerk the target path of MV further upwards, leading to an indefinite acceleration in the rate of inflation.

The right policy is somewhere between no accommodation and minimal accommodation. Where the shock is external, as with the oil price rise, there is a case for minimal accommodation so that price and wage cuts (or drastic reductions in their rate of increase) are not forced onto other sectors. But it should be made clear that there can be no financial accommodation for pay rises which attempt to recoup real income losses brought about by changed world conditions.

Even for external shocks, minimal accommodation should be reserved for very rare major and unpredicted upheavals. If every transient influence on the price level is treated as a 'shock' and demand expanded accordingly, irregular but frequent increases in monetary demand will come to be the norm and inflationary expectations will worsen with all the problems that accompany such expectations.

For domestic shocks of a wage-push kind, the general rule should be: no accommodation.[1] But, if it is to benefit rather than harm employment, it is essential for the rule to be known in advance and to carry credibility. *The hallmark of the counter-revolutionary is not a denial of the possibility of cost-push but his view of the appropriate response by policy-makers.* If domestic shocks are not accommodated, they will not, he claims, give rise to a sustained inflation (or acceleration in the inflation rate). They will certainly be costly and should be avoided as far as is within our power. But, with relatively fixed demand management rules, such explosions will generate only short-term and temporary inflationary boosts. *Above all, the knowledge that a firm demand framework exists will reduce the frequency, intensity and duration of many of these shocks.*[2]

A medium-term plan

The above line of argument leads to the proposition that the biggest contribution financial policy can make both to high employment and to low inflation is to secure a stable growth of GDP measured in money terms. A popular slogan for this objective might be 'a national cash limit'.

The central idea is that governments and central banks have a duty to try to keep the flow of total expenditure and, therefore, total income on as steady a path as possible without drastic leaps or falls The division of this growth between extra output and rising prices, i.e. between P and T, is not one that governments can influence directly. They can, however, provide a stable framework within which people can adjust their own wage and price decisions in the knowledge that they will not be bailed out of their mistakes by inflationary injections of demand.

---

[1] 'No accommodation' was recommended by the middle-of-the-road McCracken Report: *Towards Full Employment and Price Stability*, OECD, 1977. It has become almost a slogan of the OECD, although it is clearly not shared by many of the staff economists who write the country reports.

[2] This applies both to union wage push and to the secondary domestic forces by which external shocks are amplified. (This argument is taken further in the sub-section on 'Gradualism' on pp. 53-55.)

A target for Money GDP would be much easier for people to understand, once they got used to it, than the bewildering variety of money and credit measures now being canvassed, such as M1, M2, M3, 'base money', PSL_1, PSL_2, or DCE (defined in pp. 77-81). Not only that: it also provides a bridge between the more reasonable Friedmanites and the more reasonable Keynesians. For it involves retaining demand management so long as this means *monetary* demand or money times velocity (MV). It cannot mean guaranteeing *real* demand irrespective of the level of wages and prices that producer groups demand. Equally, the only reason why Friedmanites want to control the money supply is that they believe it bears a roughly stable relation to Money GDP. All they are being asked to do is to shift their headline utterances from a means to an end.

Of course, official influence over Money GDP can never be a simple progress towards straightforward targets. It involves rather the use of numbers to illustrate a general direction which is bound to be achieved jerkily. Shock events, such as the doubling of world oil prices, can push up Money GDP in the short term, which then requires patient and unpopular policies to move back on course in the way described.

The tentative 'Plan' put forward for the UK in Table II is similar in spirit to the 'Medium-Term Financial Strategy' (MTFS) inserted in the 1980 Budget over the (unfortunately not-quite-dead) body of the Bank of England and against the scepticism of even many 'Thatcherite' Ministers who believe that a week in economics is a long time. Yet it remains the sole economic innovation of that Government; and the idea deserves to be promulgated whether a particular body of politicians continues with it or not.

The main deficiency of the original 1980 MTFS was that it was stated in terms of an intermediate technical objective, 'sterling M3', rather than in terms of Money GDP which was clearly its final objective. Translated into terms of Money GDP, the Medium-Term Financial Strategy was more or less on course in the first year even though the monetary aggregates were blown sky-high. (By the winter of 1980-81 the annual growth of Money GDP had already decelerated to around 10 per cent.) My own version provides for further gradual reductions but leaves ample scope for real expansion in output if wages and prices are restrained. It was a pity that the Treasury lost an opportunity to emphasise this point, by

TABLE II

A TARGET PATH FOR MONEY GDP

		Actual	Target*
		% increase per annum	
Compound Average	1969-74	13	
,, ,,	1975-76	22	
,, ,,	1977-78	$14\frac{1}{2}$	
,, ,,	1979	15	
	1980	14	11
	1981	(10)†	10
	1982		9
	1983		8
	1984		7
	1985		6

*The targets for 1980 to 1983 inclusive are based on the Medium-Term Financial Strategy set out in the 1980 *Financial Statement and Budget Review* ('Red Book'). The sterling M3 targets have been converted into Money GDP prices by incorporating the Treasury's estimate of a 1 to 2 per cent annual increase in velocity. The strategy is carried forward a further two years.

†Forecast.

indicating only one extremely gloomy medium-term path for real output in its accompanying projections.

The main problem is the transition from one kind of régime to another. Even if output and employment would eventually be higher with fixed non-inflationary monetary and fiscal rules than in an accommodating régime, they are likely to be lower during the transition. While the credibility of a new monetary and fiscal régime is in question the economy may get the worst of all worlds, with more unemployment than under either accommodating or fixed rules. Events which shake belief in a pre-announced strategy or monetary régime without utterly destroying it are extremely expensive in terms of output and employment. The result is likely to be greater pessimism about inflation and encouragement to pressure-groups to 'have a go' with both wage claims and demands for fiscal assistance. Thus the curbs which remain depress output and employment far more than if credibility had been maintained. The advocates of retreat under fire are among the main begetters of the unemployment of which they complain.

Why not a price target?

If governments cannot spend their way into target levels of employment, why should they not aim for a price target, such as low or zero inflation? Would this not be simpler and more attractive than a target for total spending or Money GDP?

The operational counter-argument is that the price level is further removed from official influence. Control over Money GDP is itself indirect and subject to lags. But by varying the growth of monetary aggregates and the adjustment of fiscal policy, if necessary by trial and error, Money GDP can be influenced towards a target path. By contrast, the division of any increase in Money GDP between output and price changes depends on the responses of employers, trade unionists and other economic agents; and it is desirable to emphasise this very fact.

Anti-depression safeguards

There are further objections to a pure price target apart from the operational ones. Nothing has so far been said in this *Hobart Paper* to deny the possibility of fluctuations both in Money and Real GDP due to instabilities in savings or investment. Keynes's analysis of the way such instabilities can produce fluctuations in total spending remains a major achievement, rightly to be found in nearly all textbooks. These fluctuations will indeed set in train corrective forces which too many forecasting models underplay, but they may take several years to operate and there is no need to rely on them alone.

The proposal to maintain a steady growth of MV, or Money GDP, enables one to by-pass controversies about the causation of business cycles and depressions. For the effective pursuit of such a target would both prevent governments and central banks from themselves being a source of instability and also do the maximum practicable to offset fluctuations generated by the market sector through savings and investment instability or other changes in financial behaviour.

If a target for Money GDP such as that given in Table II is followed, however roughly, there simply *cannot* be a collapse of nominal income and expenditure of the kind that occurred in the USA during the Great Depression when Money GDP fell by 50 per cent between 1929 and 1933. Even in the UK it fell over the same period by 10 per cent. By contrast, it has never fallen in any post-war year up to and including 1980. An effective target for Money GDP is a re-assurance that any contractions in monetary outlays will be offset by demand-boosting policies. Moreover, whatever view one takes of gradualism, the approach also ensures that even downward deviations in the growth path are monitored and do not continue through inadvertence.

A target stated in terms of Money rather than Real GDP may be a step back from the over-reaching ambitions of recent years. It is a return not to the 1920s but to the spirit of the 1944 White Paper on *Employment Policy*,[1] hailed in its time as a revolutionary document. The White Paper's key paragraph 40 located the source of a depression in the lack of a

> 'sufficiently large expenditure on goods and services . . . The first step in a policy of maintaining general employment must be to prevent total expenditure falling away'.

The quotation is referring to expenditure in actual money, not 'real demand', 'volume terms', 'wage units', or any other kind of funny money. This is surely clear from paragraph 43 which warns that

> 'action to maintain expenditure will be fruitless unless wages and prices are kept reasonably stable'.

No kind of financial strategy can reduce the unemployment rate below the minimum consistent with a low and stable inflation rate. (This rate is labelled the CIR—constant inflation rate of unemployment—or MIR—minimum inflation rate of unemployment—and is explained fully in Section III.) All that can be expected from a financial strategy, once it has been in operation for some years, is an avoidance of unnecessary employment fluctuations and a reasonably low and stable rate of inflation. Success on these two fronts will provide a background against which underlying structural problems can be tackled with a higher chance of success.

Any businessman who has remained with me to this point waiting for a mention of the exchange rate can find some re-assurance here. For, should the effect of a high exchange rate (actual or foreseen) be so ferocious as to pull the Nominal GDP growth well below target, the strategy as formulated here would *require* the government to take action to boost

---

[1] Cmd. 6527, HMSO, 1944.

GDP, even if this meant overriding the intermediate objectives for the money supply and the PSBR. But such intervention can be justified only on the basis of total national income estimates and not of sectional grumbles by some manufacturers.

Why post-war policies worked

Another question is often asked: 'If fashionable strictures on demand management directly aimed at full employment are true, why did such policies work so well for two-and-a-half post-war decades?'. Those who ask it rarely wait for an answer.

The truth is that, for most of this period, neither the UK nor most other countries pursued demand management policies directed to full employment. The language of such policies was often used. But so long as the Bretton Woods system of exchange rates fixed against the dollar prevailed, the overriding aim was to maintain the currency parity.

Full employment demand management policies did not come to the United States until well into the 1960s. For most of the post-war period American administrations followed non-inflationary policies; and other countries, if they were to avoid devaluing against the dollar, had to imitate them. As Mr Nigel Lawson, currently Financial Secretary to the British Treasury, has written:

'During this period foreign exchange crises served as a proxy for monetary disciplines.'[1]

The policy of counter-inflation by proxy had one unfortunate legacy in the realm of ideas. It induced many people to suppose that the main obstacle to more expansionary demand policies was something called the 'balance-of-payments constraint' which, if it could be surmounted, would enable demand to be expanded to stimulate more real growth. That it would stimulate inflation instead was revealed to British governments only when the correct decision to float sterling in 1972 was accompanied by a mistaken indulgence in deficit spending and monetary expansion, with results that any Friedmanite— or, indeed, anyone schooled in the older classical tradition— would have foreseen.

By the early 1970s, the US Administration was itself pursuing highly inflationary policies, initially as a result of the

[1] *The New Conservatism,* Centre for Policy Studies, 1980.

Vietnam War and later in an effort to ensure the re-election of President Nixon. After the collapse in 1971-73 of the Bretton Woods régime of fixed exchange rates, national governments felt free to pursue purely domestic objectives. The UK was not alone but merely ahead of the field in boosting domestic demand, a policy which, followed on an international scale, produced soaring commodity prices and helped to trigger off the 1973-74 oil price explosion. It was followed by the world slump of 1974-75 and a longer-term slowdown in growth from which there is still little sign of recovery.

'Sound money' exaggerations

In most countries unemployment is now higher in boom years than it was during recession years in the 1950s and 1960s. To say (correctly) that governments were then pursuing sound money policies in disguise is to say that such policies were then consistent with full employment. But it is a mistake to go on from there to conclude that inflation is the only, or even the main, reason for the upward trend in the unemployment rate. Neither 'sound' nor 'unsound' money will restore previous employment levels if there are other forces tending to raise the minimum sustainable unemployment rate.

APPENDIX TO II

The Oil Crises

The oil price explosions of 1973-4 and 1979-80 presented peculiarly intractable problems for demand management. For they brought, in a combined package, Keynesian-type slumps in output (which reduced T) and supply shocks (which raised P). The depressive effect arose from the vast transfer of income to sparsely populated pre-industrial societies which had little need or desire to spend more than a modest proportion of their gains. The result of this transfer was a rise in the world propensity to save rather than to spend.

The published *ex-post* estimates of total OPEC surpluses (e.g. $110 billion in 1980) underestimated the contractionary effects. These occurred in a world where output and activity were already depressed. If world activity had maintained its earlier trend, total world incomes would have been larger and expenditure on oil very much larger. In that case the surpluses of the oil countries would have been far higher than anything recorded. The world recession was part of the mechanism which prevented these surpluses from being generated.

The difficulty for policy is that traditional slumps were associated with falling prices. The oil-induced depressions have been associated with a large increase in one crucial price. The direct 'knock-on' effect of the 1979-80 oil price explosion on the general price index in industrial countries has been estimated at 5 to 10 per cent,[1] without taking into account consequent wage push in an attempt to catch up with prices. The formula of maintaining a steady growth of MV would thus not have avoided the oil-induced slump in output. But a once-for-all, deliberate expansion of MV sufficient to have stopped the slump would have risked aggravating inflationary expectations and piling up problems for the future.

It is in any event extremely unlikely that OPEC producers would have been prepared to supply sufficient extra oil to maintain world activity. Attempts to boost world activity to 'normal' levels would have sent the oil price sky-high—$100 per barrel is a conservative estimate. If the industrial world had pressed on regardless with demand stimulation, OPEC producers could easily have found themselves piling up a trillion dollars per year of Western financial assets which would have been subject to enormous risks of depreciation and default. The picture is not credible. The oil would, of course, have remained in the ground, but Western economies might have collapsed in the attempt to entice it to the surface.

---

[1] *OECD Economic Outlook,* December 1980, p. 42.

III. THE SUPPLY RESPONSE

The minimum unemployment rate

More detailed discussion of the management of nominal demand will be found in Section IV. But first it is necessary to explain more fully why governments cannot spend their way into target levels of output and employment.

The most famous declamation of this proposition was made by Mr James Callaghan, then Prime Minister, in a speech to the Labour Party Conference in September 1976:

> 'We used to think that you could just spend your way out of a recession, and increase employment, by cutting taxes and boosting government spending. I tell you in all candour that that option no longer exists, and that in so far as it ever did exist, it worked by injecting inflation into the economy. And each time that happened, the average level of unemployment has risen. Higher inflation, followed by higher unemployment. That is the history of the last 20 years.'

Mr Callaghan himself quickly dropped this line of argument and by the end of the decade was passionately advancing the opposite view. Nevertheless, the original assertion, whether or not drafted by his son-in-law, Peter Jay, the former Economics Editor of *The Times*, was closer to the truth.

The basic doctrine is that there is an underlying rate of unemployment (and of output growth) which is the best that can be sustained for any period of time. It is achieved when the rate of inflation is stable and the economy has adjusted itself to it. This rate may be unsatisfactory and capable of improvement. But it can be changed only by structural reforms of markets which are working badly. Any attempt to spend ourselves into levels of employment above this sustainable rate will lead not merely to inflation but to accelerating inflation and, eventually, to a very nasty stabilisation crisis in which unemployment will shoot up to rates far higher than if the expansionary attempt had never been made.

The *minimum sustainable rate of unemployment* was labelled the 'natural rate' by Milton Friedman in his famous 1967 Presidential Address to the American Economic Association.[1] The name has eminently respectable roots; it is a deliberate analogy with Irving Fisher's 'natural rate of interest' determined by the forces of productivity and thrift, which would prevail if there was no expectation of rising or falling prices.

But the label is unfortunate since it suggests that the unemployment rate in question is normal or unavoidable. The doctrine asserts merely that it cannot be improved simply by boosting demand. It may still be far too high and capable of reduction by other kinds of policies. A better label, sometimes used in the USA, is CIR or 'constant inflation rate of unemployment'. Since that is also the minimum rate achievable by demand management, we might as well call it the MIR, which can stand for 'minimum rate of unemployment' or—to anticipate the later argument—'minimum inflation rate of unemployment'. Another possible label, suggested by Professor Richard Layard of the LSE, is the 'critical' level of unemployment.[2]

It is quite possible that union behaviour, government interferences in the labour market, bad housing policies and malfunctions of other kinds cause people to be priced out of work and that the minimum sustainable rate is wastefully high. But if the choice is between suffering high unemployment with high or low inflation, we might as well suffer it with low inflation. For this reason alone financial policies designed to achieve low and stable inflation deserve support in principle, however critical it is necessary to be of the measures employed in their pursuit.

The Phillips curve*

The notion of a minimum sustainable rate of unemployment, which cannot be reduced by boosting money flows, follows from two assumptions:

(a) that there is some sensitivity of price to demand in the labour as well as other markets;

[1] Reprinted in *The Optimum Quantity of Money*, University of Chicago Press, Chicago, 1969.

[2] Richard Layard, *Unemployment in Britain: Causes and Cures*, Discussion Paper No. 87, Centre for Labour Economics, London School of Economics, May 1981. Two further names taken from the American literature are the 'warranted rate of unemployment' and NAIR, the 'non-accelerating inflation rate of unemployment'.

(b) that no major group can be systematically tricked by inflation into accepting a lower share of the national product.[1]

There is no need to assume that labour demand is the only or even the principal influence on wages, but merely that it is an influence. It was for a long time customary to depict this influence by the single curve in the upper figure of Chart 2. Such a curve was fitted by the late Professor A. W. Phillips to British data for 1861-1913 and also for the post-war period to 1957.[2] The suggested relationship became known as the 'Phillips curve'. It led policy-makers to assume that they had a menu of choices between different combinations of unemployment and inflation—an assumption which still bedevils much political discussion.

No sooner had the Phillips curve become part of the applied economist's stock-in-trade than it began to be alarmingly misleading. It had always been difficult to fit the curve to countries other than the USA and the UK. Even in these two countries, from the late 1960s onwards unemployment rates which were very high by post-war standards came to be associated with double-digit inflation rates. Conversely, toleration of rapid inflation did not bring the low unemployment that a simple reading of the curve would suggest.

It is not difficult to see why the Phillips curve should shift. It was fitted for a period when there were expectations either of stable prices or of a stable and predictable upward creep.

Chart 2 illustrates the processes at work. It is best to begin by concentrating on the simple upper figure, which postulates a relationship between wage increases and unemployment. A zero increase in productivity is assumed purely to simplify the arithmetic (the removal of the assumption does not change the argument).

---

[1] These common-sense assertions should not be confused with technical arguments about the neutrality of money. Even an inflation which is perfectly anticipated, and to which everyone has adjusted, will affect holdings of real money balances, bonds and physical capital and, therefore, the distribution of income. Inflation will be strictly neutral only if the excess money is issued in the form of payment of interest on cash balances. (J. Niehans, *The Theory of Money*, Johns Hopkins University Press, Baltimore, Maryland, 1978, p. 28.) All that is asserted here is that people will not behave indefinitely as if they did not realise that inflation was occurring or changing in speed.

[2] 'The Relationship between Unemployment and the Rate of Change of Money Wages in the UK, 1861-1957', *Economica*, 1958, pp. 783-91; reprinted in R. J. Ball and P. Doyle (eds.), *Inflation*, Penguin Books, 1969.

CHART 2

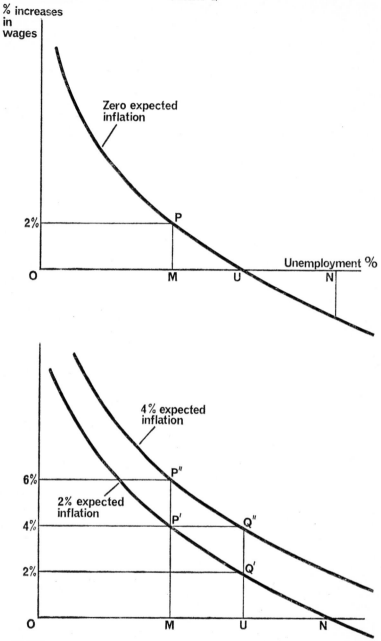

Phillips curves under varying expected rates of inflation

We also assume a constant percentage mark-up on wages for all products and constant terms of trade—again for simplicity. Then the rate of increase of wages is the same as the rate of increase of prices and represents the inflation rate. There is one unemployment rate, OU, at which there is no increase in average wages and at which inflation is zero.

What happens if the government finds OU too high and tries to boost demand? So long as 'money illusion' reigns— that is, workers take no notice of inflation in their bargaining behaviour—the story need go no further. Lower unemployment will have been purchased at the expense of some inflation. The economy is at point P on the upper figure of Chart 2. Unemployment has fallen to OM, but inflation has risen from zero to 2 per cent.

Unfortunately this is only the first stage. Sooner or later 'money illusion' disappears and workers begin to think in real terms. They start insisting on still higher wages to make up for the rise in the cost of living. The economy is then at point P' on the lower curve of the bottom figure of Chart 2. (This is known as an expectations-augmented Phillips curve, because it incorporates the expectation that prices will rise by 2 per cent.) Workers now ask for a 4 per cent wage increase to make up for the fact that prices are rising by 2 per cent and have eroded their initial gains. But once they obtain these new increases, prices too will rise by 4 per cent. Before long the expected rate of inflation rises to 4 per cent, in line with actual inflation, and the economy shifts onto the still higher inflation-augmented Phillips curve passing through point P''.

Once that happens workers will demand 6 per cent wage increases and, so long as demand is kept up, employers will concede it. This in turn will give the prices spiral a further twist leading to larger and larger wage and price increases following each other indefinitely. So long as unemployment is held down at OM by government demand boosts, inflation will continue to accelerate. Thus the long-run trade-off is not between unemployment and inflation, with which we might try to live, but between unemployment and accelerating inflation. As a monetary economy cannot survive without a viable form of money, the acceleration will eventually have to be brought to an end.

In this example, Ministers and central bankers are faced with a painful dilemma. If they try to keep unemployment at the lower level OM by ever larger financial injections, they face the eventual collapse of the national monetary unit as a basis for business calculations—and with it the end to any benefit to employment from their policies—not to speak of the political and social repercussions of currency collapse. If, before this stage is reached, they try to return to the inflation rate at which they began their experiment (zero in our example), unemployment may have to shoot temporarily well *above* OU, the long-term minimum. This is because of the difficulty of reducing inflationary expectations once they have become embedded in the economic system.

Should the government be prepared to settle for whatever rate of inflation has emerged when it abandons its demand-boosting experiment, it will have to allow unemployment to return to at least OU; and some time will elapse before the system settles down at the newly-chosen position. Thus the long-term Phillips curve is a vertical line going through U, Q' and Q'' in the lower figure, and there is no long-term choice between unemployment and inflation.

The unique point of stability is that corresponding to the sustainable level of unemployment, OU. At that level wage increases will neither climb above nor fall below price increases. At any point on UQ' Q'' the rate of inflation will be stable, but it can be stable at 0, 2, 20 or 200 per cent inflation. Thus, ultimately, the rate of growth of monetary demand affects only the inflation rate, the effects on employment being transitory.

The strict logic of this analysis would suggest that deflationary policies designed to drive unemployment *above* OU would eventually produce continuously *falling* wages and prices. But it is doubtful if inflationary and deflationary processes are symmetrical in today's circumstances since wages are more resistant to downward than to upward pressures. At the very least, the speed of adjustment may be slower in the face of abnormally low demand for labour than in the face of abnormally high demand.

Keynesian demand deficiency can be interpreted as a situation in which the economy is on one of the Phillips curves at a point to the right of OU. The function of demand management is then to return the economy to OU faster than natural processes will achieve. *The assertion of the counter-revolutionaries is that OU cannot be improved upon by demand management alone.*

Chart 2 is, of course, highly schematic. The government can

hardly experiment with different unemployment rates. In practice, many other things will be happening at the same time. OU might itself shift, and expectations about policy will influence the speed and character of the whole process. The inflation-augmented Phillips curve is nevertheless a useful device. It shows, for instance, what is wrong with the popular 'sound money' argument that any degree of inflation is bound to accelerate. It is not. Inflation can remain indefinitely at, for instance, Q′ or Q″, provided that the country's rulers are prepared to settle for the sustainable unemployment rate OU. But politically it is probable that the impulses (such as the desire to reduce unemployment to OM) which led to the initial inflation will produce policies that culminate in successively higher inflation rates. Eventually, disillusionment may set in; or the reaction may speed up so much that the temporary employment gain is eliminated.[1]

Chart 2 also demonstrates the fallacy behind the popular question: 'What is to stop inflation re-starting once the squeeze has come to an end?' The mistake is to confuse the unemployment cost of *reducing* inflation with the cost of a *permanently lower* rate of inflation. The squeeze is represented by the excess unemployment UN. Once inflation has fallen to the desired rate unemployment can safely fall back to OU (i.e. the sustainable rate) without any inflationary effect.

Will inflation return?

Inflation need not return to its old level after a squeeze because the rate of price rises which workers fear and the rate which employers are able to pay are now much lower. So both the wage increases which workers desire—in a given state of the labour market and with given union power—and the increases which employers can afford to offer are lower than before. If

[1] So long as there remain any lags at all in reaction to excess demand, observers are likely to overestimate the effective capacity ceiling or 'overheating point' of the economy. Let us suppose that the demand for labour is raised along the curve in the upper figure of Chart 2 to point P. It may take up to a year for the tightening of the labour market to affect wages by the full amount PM. It will then look as if the point of overheating is P, whereas it is really any point to the left of U.

The same effect works in reverse. If demand is restricted and unemployment raised to N as part of the counter-inflation policy, it will look as if unemployment ON is the 'price' of low inflation. In fact it is only the price of reducing the inflation rate. Once inflation has fallen by the desired amount, unemployment can decline to OU without provoking a fresh inflationary surge.

[41]

inflation does embark on a consistent acceleration, it is a sign that the government has been over-optimistic about the CIR and is trying to run the economy at a higher pressure than is sustainable without more fundamental reforms in the economic structure.

It cannot be over-emphasised that there is no need for the government to estimate the CIR directly, and that it is even dangerous for it to try. If its financial policy concentrates on maintaining a stable growth of monetary demand, the economy will settle at (or fluctuate around) the CIR. Indeed, this is the most effective way to discover how high the CIR is.

The argument that any trade-off between inflation and unemployment vanishes in the long term (i.e. that there is a vertical long-run Phillips curve) is occasionally met by the claim that wages respond to the rate of change of unemployment and not to its level. Both are important. But as long as the level matters too, the influence of the rate of change of unemployment will be to cause overshooting and undershooting, and not to overthrow the basic relationship.[1]

It is sometimes argued that wage gains from inflationary policies will not be completely eroded since profit margins may be reduced.[2] If so, the argument that demand-boosting policies are ineffective in reducing unemployment for more than a temporary period is strengthened. For, in those circumstances, unemployment will not merely fail to register an enduring fall but will actually rise. A squeeze on margins means that real wages have increased for employers in terms of their own product. They will respond to higher labour costs as to higher costs of any other input, by switching to methods and lines of production of a more labour-saving kind. Thus a boost to

---

[1] If the rate of change of unemployment were alone relevant to inflation, we would have to ask at what rate of change of unemployment inflation would be stable. If this rate were positive, unemployment would have to rise continuously, which is absurd. If it were negative, unemployment would have to fall continuously, which is also absurd. But suppose the equilibrium rate of change is zero. Then, when unemployment is stable, inflation is also stable. This implies that the rate of inflation could be anything at all, irrespective of the state of the labour market, which is again hard to believe.

None of this is to deny that we are in for a rough ride if, in the actual range in which the economy is working, the effects of the rate of change of unemployment are important relatively to the level of unemployment.

[2] It is extremely unlikely that import prices could be prevented from rising, for this would imply that a country could permanently improve its terms of trade with the rest of the world by inflation.

monetary demand associated with falling margins and higher real wages is worse from the point of view of unemployment than one in which all costs and prices are marked up in proportion.

*More classical approaches**

There are many different ways of arriving at the concept of a minimum sustainable unemployment rate (which, in terms of Chart 2, amounts to a vertical long-run Phillips curve). In the above exposition the causal link runs from unemployment to wages and prices, as in the work of Professor David Laidler[1] and of many other counter-revolutionaries who started off as Keynesians.

But for some economists of a more purely classical way of thinking, including Milton Friedman, the link is the other way round—from wages and prices to employment. The rise in employment and output comes about because people mistake an inflationary increase in prices and wages generally for an improvement in the market for their own product. This induces them to offer more hours of work and put more goods on the market, which they later withdraw on realising they have mistaken the general inflation for a specific improvement in the market price of their own product. Recognition dawns when they find that they are not obtaining improved real wages and profits, and begin to take inflation into account in evaluating their own apparent gains.

Conversely, when inflation is reduced, employment and output are withdrawn because people mistakenly interpret a general deceleration of inflation as a deterioration in the rewards of their own industry. On this model, unemployment occurs because people fail to perceive what is happening to the general price level.

Thus there are two very different stories about the exact route by which an injection of increased monetary demand first stimulates output and employment and is then eroded by faster

[1] [David E. W. Laidler was Professor of Economics at the University of Manchester from 1969 to 1976, and has been Professor of Economics at the University of Western Ontario since 1976. He has written numerous books and papers on aspects of monetary theory and policy. He contributed a 'British Commentary' to Milton Friedman's *Unemployment versus Inflation? An Evaluation of the Phillips Curve*, Occasional Paper 44, IEA, 1975; and a Memorandum, 'Notes on Gradualism', to the *Memoranda on Monetary Policy* submitted to the Treasury and Civil Service Committee (HC720, HMSO, 1980).—ED.]

inflation. There are still further versions: both the ones given so far would be regarded as intellectually dated by a recent group of theorists known as the 'new neo-classical school'.[1]

Fortunately for the purposes of policy, the doctrine of the minimum sustainable or 'natural' rate of unemployment—and the (at best temporary) effects of demand boosts intended to reduce it—is compatible with a great many different ideas about the detailed underlying process. It is, for instance, compatible with wages being set by collective bargaining, with union monopoly power, and with labour markets which are not cleared, i.e. remain in surplus or shortage for considerable periods. Indeed, my own exposition was deliberately conducted in terms appropriate to such institutions.

Nor does the CIR doctrine depend on the view that all individuals are rational maximisers, or that unemployment is voluntary, or that the degree of monopoly power exercised by individual unions is constant or stable. Changes in union militancy may alter the CIR. For the CIR to exist it is only necessary for both sides of the labour market to be sensitive to demand conditions and not to be deluded indefinitely by changes in the rate of inflation.

Fine-tuning*

Despite the assertions of the former Prime Minister, Mr James Callaghan, governments could in principle spend their way out of a *recession*—if a recession is defined as unemployment *above* the CIR or 'natural' rate (higher than OU in Chart 2) and self-correcting forces act too slowly. In principle, if governments knew enough, they could reduce fluctuations in unemployment and activity around the minimum sustainable—or so-called 'natural'—rate of unemployment.

Critics of fine-tuning are sceptical of government's ability to perform even this limited function. Their original attack on fine-tuning and discretionary demand management emphasised the lags between the occurrence of a fluctuation, its diagnosis, the subsequent policy decisions, their implementation and their ultimate impact. The effect of these lags could be so great that would-be stabilisation measures might actually aggravate the fluctuations they were intended to reduce.

[1] The works of Professor Patrick Minford and associates at the University of Liverpool mentioned in the Select Bibliography (page 129) provide a useful introduction to that school.

This criticism, which was at the heart of the original debate over 'stop-go', is probably still valid. But the main danger of fine-tuning based on short-term forecasts is different, namely, that it is all too likely to embody an over-optimistic idea of the CIR, or sustainable level of output and employment. Thus attempts at fine-tuning may not merely accentuate fluctuations in employment and inflation but lead to accelerating inflation, followed by a crisis and a violent stop.

The CIR is too unstable (and, therefore, too difficult to estimate) to be used directly for fine-tuning purposes or for economic management in general. Indeed, it would be a mistake to expect very much stability in forces such as union use of monopoly power, structural shifts in world demand, and perceived political and financial uncertainties, all of which influence the level of the CIR.

The costs of inflation

Inflation itself has an unemployment cost. The long-term Phillips curve may thus not be vertical but positively sloped, with more inflation bringing more unemployment—the opposite of the trade-off originally postulated.

Even stable and anticipated inflation extracts a high price in what J. Niehans aptly calls 'accounting costs'.[1] Under rapid inflation, he writes,

> 'in all his planning for the future, including insurance, pension plans, savings, mortgages and the like, the consumer would be involved in almost continuous compound interest computations, either absorbing considerable time, skill and/or equipment or else resulting in error'.

The passions and confusions in Britain today arising from indexed pensions in the public (government) sector are an illustration. Even a large business has to be very careful that it has not been misled by inflation into consuming capital in the guise of profits. Niehans cites

> 'the resources that have gone into writing, reading, debating and to some extent even applying the inflation accounting literature. It is also agreed that the practical results are quite imperfect'.

High inflation brings with it high nominal interest rates. Real interest rates (i.e. adjusted for inflation) need be no higher; and

---

[1] *The Theory of Money, op. cit.*, p. 70.

TABLE III

CASH OUTFLOWS—LOAN OF £100 FOR FIVE YEARS

| | Zero real interest rate | |
	Zero inflation	20 per cent inflation
Year 1	0	20*
Year 2	0	20
Year 3	0	20
Year 4	0	20
Year 5	100	120

*Even though the real interest rate is zero, the borrower has to start making substantial payments in the first year when there is inflation.

some of the cruder complaints against high interest rates overlook the fact that the borrower will repay in depreciated currency. Nevertheless, high nominal interest rates do cause major problems for business and personal borrowers alike. They are of two main varieties, the cash flow problem and the risk problem. The cash flow problem is illustrated in Table III. A loan of £100 for five years is considered; and to make the arithmetic simple, the real rate of interest is assumed to be zero. If there is no inflation the borrower pays nothing for the first four years and returns £100 at the end of the fifth year.

Now assume that inflation is 20 per cent and that the nominal rate of interest has risen to 20 per cent too. The borrower's outgoings are shown in the second column as £20 per annum, except for the fifth year when he has to repay the original £100 as well, making an outlay of £120 in that year. The real cost of the loan is still zero. His £100 repayment is worth approximately £40 in the money of the beginning of the period; and the annual £20 'interest payments' are in actuality advance repayments of principal.

Nevertheless the borrower may have a severe cash flow problem. In the zero inflation case he has no outgoings until the end of the fifth year. But when inflation and nominal interest rates are 20 per cent he has to start making advance repayments straight away, which are most onerous in the first year. These high initial outgoings are known as the problem of 'front loading' and are familiar to every house purchaser in the early stages of a mortgage. They have to be financed either from existing earnings or by fresh borrowing. Such borrowing makes both creditor and debtor uneasy. It can even run into legal difficulties since corporate articles of association and debenture agreements sometimes limit new borrowing and are drawn up in a way which makes no allowance for inflation.

The second problem is the risk that inflation will change. In practice, rapid inflation is also highly variable, its rate being difficult to predict. Annual rates of UK inflation, for instance, have fluctuated between 6 and 24 per cent since 1970. If someone borrows at a fixed rate of interest of 20 per cent when inflation is at that rate, then, if inflation were to fall to zero, his real rate of interest as well as his nominal one would become 20 per cent. (No wonder the debenture market dried up in the UK in the 1970s.) Both the cash flow distortions and the additional risks imposed by high nominal interest rates were emphasised very heavily by the Wilson Committee.[1]

Rapid inflation thus tends to shorten time-horizons and militates against risk-taking investment. More generally, the vital signalling function of market prices is weakened. Price or wage changes which would normally signal surpluses, shortages, and the existence of profitable opportunities become difficult to distinguish from general inflationary movements. The evidence suggests that adaptation and indexation, always imperfect, face more obstacles in large economies with extensive financial institutions, such as those of North America and North West Europe, than in, say, Israel or Iceland or even Brazil. When market signals break down and short-term horizons dominate, it is highly probable that unused resources and unsatisfied demands will exist side by side and that part of the real income loss will appear in extra unemployment.

But perhaps the worst effect of rapid inflation is to tempt politicians to resort to price controls (also mentioned in the Wilson Report) and tailor economic policy to buy union support for wage restraint. The 1980 Brookings Report on the UK[2] suggests a line of causation from inflation to union militancy—the reverse of what is normally assumed. Unionisation is likely to spread during periods of high and uncertain inflation

---

[1] *Committee to Review the Functioning of Financial Institutions*, Cmnd. 7937, HMSO, 1980, especially para. 482 and Chapter 17.

[2] Richard E. Caves and Lawrence B. Krause (eds.), *Britain's Economic Performance*, The Brookings Institution, Washington DC, 1980.

as more and more people become dependent on organised pay bargaining to maintain their place in the pecking order.

The meaning of price stability

Historically, periods of price stability were not ones of zero price change. Year-to-year price variations ran to several per cent; and there were decades at a time of what would nowadays be called 'creeping' inflation or deflation. The difference from today is that the direction of movement was unknowable. Prices were as likely to fall as to rise. Stability was therefore the best predictive bet; deviations from it were not so big as to destroy a person's savings, and were in any case likely to be reversed in a single lifetime.

The result was a combination of basic stability with modest short-term flexibility. If a country's terms of trade deteriorated, or if there was a harvest failure, or if real national income fell for any other reason, the burden would be spread automatically through a temporary rise in the price level without any painful re-negotiation of contracts. On the other hand, pensions could be arranged on the basis that a pound was a pound and a dollar a dollar; and wage negotiators would not be forced to add an uncertain inflation premium to their offers and demands.

The situation was in marked contrast to the post-war period and especially the most recent decades when inflation has been high and variable and people have had to work with a shrinking monetary yardstick. This makes all business calculations a gamble and causes anyone who relies on a fixed money pension to pray he will not live too long.

Alternatively, indexation is introduced throughout the economy, thereby easing some of the inflationary distortions discussed above. But unless the indexation is carried out very carefully, the safety-valve of rising prices, which reduce real incomes in adverse economic circumstances, is removed; and there is a danger of appearing to guarantee to the population more than the entire value of the national income. An example of the wrong sort of indexation is an escalation clause like the Italian *scala mobile*, which automatically compensates wage earners for inflation. A sensible form of wage indexation would allow for the possibility of real wages going down as well as up in accordance with the market pressures of the time. Both indexation and non-indexation are thus in practice unsatisfactory

[48]

alternatives. Although in my view carefully introduced indexation is an essential second best in inflationary times, and can even be an adjunct to anti-inflationary policies,[1] there will be no satisfactory solution until inflation itself has been brought down to a low or zero rate.

The transmission mechanism*

To summarise: Professor Phillips achieved fame and notoriety by suggesting a trade-off between inflation and unemployment. The counter-revolutionaries at first accepted that the trade-off existed in the short run, but argued that either there was no trade-off at all in the longer run or, if there was, that it was perverse, with inflation inducing more unemployment rather than less. Much has, however, happened to give a new slant to the counter-revolution since it first emerged at the end of the 1960s and the beginning of the 1970s. These developments have cast doubt on whether there is even a favourable *short-term* trade-off.

In Europe, although not in the USA, consumers responded to the higher inflation of the 1970s by increasing their savings ratios. They did so in an effort to offset the erosion of financial assets of given face value, such as savings deposits and government securities. It was next observed that, in medium-sized European countries (but now increasingly in the USA as well), the foreign exchange market short-circuited the domestic labour market. The immediate effect of domestic monetary expansion with a floating exchange rate is depreciation of the currency (other things being equal). This causes domestic prices to rise much more quickly than would occur with purely domestic transmission from a tighter labour market to higher wage increases.

In this model, which Professors Ball, Burns and Budd were instrumental in developing at the London Business School, the key variable is the world rate of inflation. Excessive monetary and fiscal expansion in the industrial countries leads to an acceleration in commodity prices even before the rate of wage increases starts to rise. Each country will share in, or contract out of, world inflation according to the behaviour of its exchange rate.

[1] Outlined by Milton Friedman in *Monetary Correction* (sub-titled 'A proposal for escalator clauses to reduce the costs of ending inflation'), Occasional Paper 41, IEA, 1974.

CHART 3

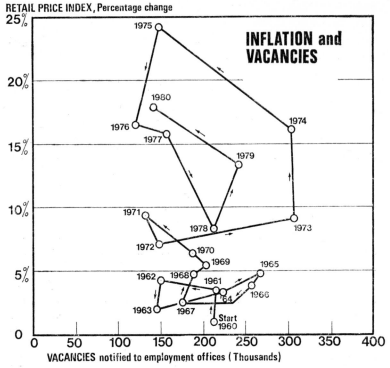

RETAIL PRICE INDEX, Percentage change

INFLATION and VACANCIES

VACANCIES notified to employment offices (Thousands)

The economy has moved in a series of 'Phillips loops'. In the first 'worst of all worlds' phase after the introduction of restrictive financial policies, or an outside financial shock, the demand for labour (shown by unfilled vacancies) falls, but inflation continues to increase (as in 1979-80). In the second 'recession' phase vacancies continue to fall, but inflation falls too. In the third 'fool's paradise' phase inflation falls, but vacancies rise. In the fourth 'overheating' phase vacancies continue to fall, but overheating leads to rising inflation. Sooner or later restrictive measures are taken and the cycle begins again.

This approach also focusses on the prices of domestic assets such as houses and land, which respond quickly to demand influences well before wages, and before the prices of newly produced goods and services.

The net result of all these short-circuits is that the effect on prices of an expansionary demand policy can come through much more quickly *via* routes other than the labour market one; and the more quickly higher demand spills over into prices the less there is left over to boost output and employment, even temporarily.

CHART 4

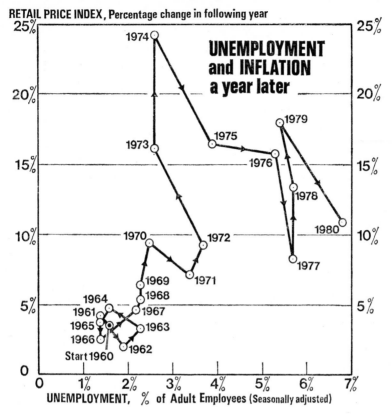

RETAIL PRICE INDEX, Percentage change in following year

UNEMPLOYMENT and INFLATION a year later

UNEMPLOYMENT, % of Adult Employees (Seasonally adjusted)

It is prudent, however, to retain some agnosticism about the transmission mechanism. Conditions vary from one period to another. When inflation falls people are likely to save less because of the rise in the value of their financial assets. But, if unemployment is also rising, they may save more for precautionary reasons; and it is dangerous to generalise about which effect will predominate in a particular year.

Recent experience suggests a certain asymmetry in the transmission process. In other words, expansionary monetary and fiscal policies based on an over-optimistic view of the CIR feed very quickly into higher inflation. Restrictive policies, on the other hand, still work in the old-fashioned way: first they induce a recession and then they reduce inflation, with output recovering some time later, as depicted in Charts 3 and 4.

[51]

The most general influence on the speed of transmission is expectations. Once people expect a higher budget deficit or rapid monetary expansion to lead to more inflation, the effect can come through very quickly indeed as the exchange rate and gilt-edged prices are marked down, earnings are pushed up, and so on.

Crucial to expectations is the policy régime believed to be in operation. On the down side, for instance, if price and wage setters believe that monetary and fiscal guidelines are here to stay, they will adjust much more quickly—both because they have become more optimistic about inflation and because they are more fearful of pricing their products and members out of their markets. This, in a nutshell, is the case for medium-term targets, together with action to underpin their credibility. By contrast, if the targets are fixed for only a short period at a time and there is a general belief that they will be missed, or adjusted upwards at the first sign of recession, people will quite rationally refrain from changing their wage and price behaviour. Then the effects of monetary restraint will for quite a time be almost exclusively on output and employment.[1]

These remarks embody many of the policy insights of the 'rational expectations' school of thought. Signed-up members will, of course, go a good deal further and assert that people adapt very quickly to new conditions in setting wages and prices, and that only *unexpected* changes in policy or unexpected news can affect output and employment. This does not mean that people adjust instantaneously to new monetary and fiscal guidelines. They may for good reasons be uncertain what the policy means or whether it will be observed. Furthermore, the existence of previous contracts inhibits instantaneous adjustment.

The most controversial version of the doctrine asserts that people act 'as if' they have correct knowledge of economic relationships; or, somewhat more plausibly, that they do not make systematic mistakes in predicting inflation (or valuing shares) which policy-makers or forecasters can exploit.

For the purposes of this *Paper* it is unnecessary to reach a firm view about any of these ideas which are 'under research'.

---

[1] An eloquent exposition of this point is in the 1981 *Annual Report* of President Carter's outgoing Council of Economic Advisers, US Government Printing Office, DC 20402, p. 44 *et seq.*

The key point is never to forget the rôle of expectations. The initial unemployment cost of counter-inflation is exacerbated by uncertainty about longer-term policy or lack of credibility for announced intentions.

'Gradualism'*

The new emphasis on expectations sheds light on the issue of gradualism. The original theory of gradualism was based on a fairly straightforward interpretation of the relationships shown in Chart 2 (p. 38). These suggest there is a minimum sustainable rate of unemployment consistent with any *constant* rate of inflation (which was called the CIR), but that, if the government wants to reduce the rate of inflation, a period of abnormally high unemployment (above the CIR) is required.

It was to limit the transitional unemployment and recession cost of an anti-inflation programme that Friedman and others originally suggested aiming initially at a rate of monetary growth just below that appropriate to the current rate of inflation and reducing it gradually until inflation was eliminated or reduced to whatever rate a country was prepared to accept.

A mechanistic application of this doctrine can produce treacherous results. Suppose there is a target path for the growth of monetary demand of 11 per cent for the first year, 10 per cent for the second, 9 per cent for the third, and so on. It can happen that, while these targets are being formulated, a series of shocks—such as an oil price increase, a shift from income tax to VAT, or a public sector wage explosion following the breakdown of official wage controls—temporarily lifts the rate of inflation to 20 per cent. The real squeeze will then be much more severe than originally intended. On the other hand, if the monetary target is adjusted upwards with each such shock, inflation will move upwards in a ratchet process (as explained in the section on shocks, pp. 25-27).

Quite apart from such shocks, mechanistic calculations of how much excess unemployment will accompany a reduction in inflation by a given amount are profoundly misguided. An example is the 'conclusion' of the House of Commons Select Committee on the Treasury and Civil Service that to reduce inflation permanently by 1 per cent would cost the equivalent of $2\frac{1}{2}$ per cent excess unemployment (above the CIR) maintained for four years.[1] The point about such calculations is not that they are pessimistic but that they are misconceived and systematically mislead the politicians they are designed to help.

The unemployment cost arises because it takes time for people's expectations, long-term contracts and administrative and business customs to adjust to a lower rate of inflation. But once they have done so there is no need for the $2\frac{1}{2}$ per cent extra slack (if that is really the amount) to remain to achieve further reductions in the rate of inflation. The emphasis on expectations suggests that the return to the CIR, or normal rate of unemployment, may take place long before a gradualist counter-inflation programme is completed. Once the crucial breakthrough has been made, the cost of reducing inflation by 10 per cent a year may be nothing like ten times as high as that of reducing it by 1 per cent.

It is vital not to erect a rival mechanistic dogma to replace that of the Treasury Committee. It cannot be gaily said that a government should seek to reduce inflation from 20 per cent to zero in one fell policy change, even if there was a willingness to be stoical about the costs in the first year or two. Adjustment and adaptation are not matters of black and white, yes or no. Suppose, for instance, that the initial 20 per cent inflation is unusually high and regarded as an aberration, but that on the other hand there has been no experience of single digit inflation for more than a decade. Then it might be relatively easy to reduce inflationary expectations to about 10 per cent or just below, but extremely difficult to reduce them further to 5 per cent or zero.

The impact of long-established contracts is also exceedingly complex. A rapid reduction in inflation will raise the real value of money balances, savings accounts and fixed interest securities. The result will be to bolster personal consumption and thus help output and employment. On the other hand, it will raise the burden on companies of servicing long-term loans. Again, different effects will predominate at different rates of inflation.

Quite apart from whether it is desirable, a gradualist counter-inflation policy is very difficult to administer in prac-

---

[1] Third Report from the Treasury and Civil Service Committee, Session 1980-81, *Monetary Policy*, Vol. I: *Report*, House of Commons Paper 163—I, HMSO, 1981, para. 11. 17.

tice. A gradualist path for intermediate targets, such as the monetary aggregates and the PSBR, does not necessarily mean gradualism in impact, even if the intended path can be observed. There are likely to be no effects for quite a while; and then suddenly there is a sharp and delayed catching-up as stocks are run down and lay-offs announced. This path of events was associated in the UK in 1979-80 with a rise in the exchange rate which made the demand squeeze much sharper than expected or intended. But the first rule of political economy, as of politics in general, is that the 'unexpected' often happens. When it does, it is sensible to accept it. Once inflation has fallen faster than predicted, it is advisable to take the new lower rate of inflation as a starting point for demand management. An attempt to return to the original path by raising monetary demand risks rekindling inflationary expectations, in which event the sacrifices will have been in vain and further periods of excess unemployment will be required before the original inflation target is eventually reached.

Constraints on output

Both sides in the argument between the post-war establishment and the counter-revolutionaries have located the constraint on output in the labour market. This largely reflects experience up to 1973, but the constraint can first reveal itself in other markets, as experience since that year demonstrates.

During a boom, commodity prices can start to accelerate on a world scale earlier and more vigorously than wages. Another example of a non-labour constraint is found in the developing countries. In many of them there is not enough capital or enterprise to employ available workers at wages above subsistence. In such countries excessive demand expansion will manifest itself in the goods rather than the labour market, with higher prices, shortages and increased imports as evidence.

Another and highly topical example of a constraint on output, arising from outside the labour market, is the limitation of oil supplies. Indeed, the oil supply position may now be the main brake on the growth of output in the industrial world as a whole. Because of the limited need for higher revenue of some of the main oil-exporting countries, the supply of oil may, for the time being, be insensitive to price. Thus, if an attempt is made to boost world demand, the main effect could be a multiple increase in oil prices with very little increase in supplies and very little increase in world output.

The oil constraint has tended to be forgotten in times of recession such as 1975-76 or in 1981 but has an ugly habit of re-appearing just when the world economy has regained an upward path. An individual country can escape this constraint by increasing its share of world output, but the world as a whole cannot. The oil constraint will not be there for ever. The rise in the real price of oil will in time stimulate the development of new sources of energy and of energy-saving techniques. It is mentioned here as an example of one of the many types of supply constraint which help to determine the maximum rate of growth of output that it is possible to achieve without running into accelerating inflation.

Thus, the theory of a sustainable rate of unemployment is a stepping stone to the more general idea of a sustainable rate of growth of output, irrespective of the nature of the constraint. Persistent attempts to expand monetary demand above the sustainable growth rate will lead to accelerating inflation, and the bottlenecks can be in any market.

The constraint is not always a physical one. World expansion could continue despite rising commodity prices if workers in consuming countries accepted the consequent deterioration in their terms of trade. Overheating in a boom can develop well before physical reserves of labour or other factors of production come to an end. It develops when the required factors can be brought into operation only by a level of real rewards which more than exhausts the total national product.

The key questions to ask about any increase in nominal demand are:

(a) What will be the supply response?

(b) What effect will it have on price expectations?

The two are, of course, related. For if a 1 per cent increase in nominal demand is expected to raise prices by 1 per cent, any effect on output will be at most transitory, enduring only so long as contracts made at the old price level remain in force. If major inflationary injections become part of the normal order of things, contracts will soon become formally or informally re-negotiable.

Unemployment and Inflation

'Can you give us a clear and definite statement of the relationship between unemployment and inflation?' The accompanying Chart 5 attempts to do so. (In contrast to Chart 2, unemployment is plotted against price rather than wage increases. It is thus assumed that, if wages increase faster, so will prices by an amount related to the gross mark-up.)

Its message is that there *is* a *short-run* trade-off. A reduction in inflation will normally require a period of abnormally high unemployment. An increase in inflation may be accompanied by a temporary fall in unemployment—but this is much less certain (hence the abbreviated cut-off nature of the left-hand portion of the short-term Phillips curves).

In the long run, however, there is either no relation at all, or—at very high rates of inflation—an opposite relation. That is, very high rates of inflation are associated with high rates of unemployment. (In other words, the Phillips curve is positively sloped.)

Thus, OQo in Chart 5 is near the MIR, the minimum rate of unemployment which can be achieved without fundamental structural change. The 'constant inflation' (or 'natural') rate of unemployment now becomes a range, with OQo near the lower limit.

The short-term Phillips curve shows that the initial stages of an anti-inflationary programme will lead to a temporary rise in unemployment. There is, however, no simple proportional relationship between the size of the reduction in inflation and either the amount or the duration of the extra unemployment.

The steps by which the economy moves from the short-term to the long-term Phillips curve will vary widely according to the particular circumstances of each cycle. Charts 3 and 4 in the preceding sub-sections show what has happened in some recent cycles.

Chart 5 is meant to give merely a schematic presentation. The indicated rates of inflation represent rough guesses about orders of magnitude. The short term is a year or two for practical purposes. (Over still shorter periods anything can happen, depending on the starting point and immediate past history.) The long run is defined as the period over which the economy has adjusted to the prevailing rate of inflation. Three to seven years may be typical for the bulk of the adjustment. But the speed of adjustment is probably faster with increases than with decreases in the rate of inflation. It is certainly higher today than it used to be in the 1950s and 1960s.

A steady rate of inflation of 20, 30 or 50 per cent is unknown, and probably impossible. Thus the higher reaches of the long-run Phillips curve are best regarded as representing averages around

[57]

CHART 5

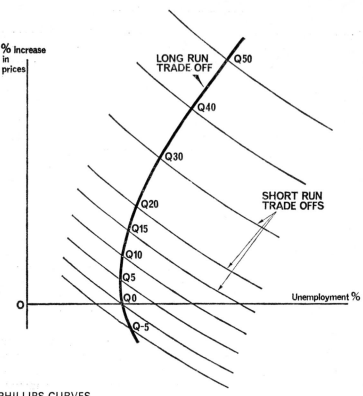

PHILLIPS CURVES

The points labelled Q are the points on the short-term Phillips curve where the expected rate of inflation is equal to the actual rate. At Q0 these rates are both 0, at Q5 they are both 5%, at Q10 they are both 10% etc., at Q–5 they are both minus 5%; i.e. there is both expected and actual deflation.

The thin curves indicate the short-run trade-offs; the thick curve the long-run trade-offs.

Hypothetical unemployment/inflation trade-off

which the rate of inflation oscillates. A large part of the long-run unemployment costs arises from the instability and unpredictability of actual rates of inflation when the average rate is high.

There are some vital qualifications to be made. Chart 5 represents changes emanating only from the demand (or MV) side, whether induced by government policy or by changes in private sector financial behaviour.

There are many forces on the supply (PT) side which can boost prices in the short term and also raise unemployment, thus giving a perverse trade-off even in the short term. Obvious examples are the oil price explosions of 1973-74 and 1979-80. Many events and policies will also raise unemployment without even a temporary, favourable effect on inflation. An increase in union monopoly power, or a worsening of the 'poverty trap', will shift the long-term Phillips curve to the right and worsen unemployment with no reduction in inflation even in the short term.

The main lessons of Chart 5 are negative. Any fall in unemployment resulting from inflationary policies is at best temporary; 'eliminating inflation' cannot in most normal circumstances be relied upon to make a large permanent dent in unemployment, although it is likely to do some good.

IV. INSTRUMENTS AND OBJECTIVES

Subordinate guidelines

There is no hard-and-fast line between means and ends. Economic growth, high employment and price stability are themselves means to the maximisation of economic welfare, utility or whatever other label is fashionable for ultimate economic objectives. These objectives are themselves means of greater or lesser importance to whatever higher ideals of personal or human advancement people happen to hold.

The art of policy is to specify the objectives which are crucial for the purpose in hand. It has been argued above that a stable growth of monetary demand (i.e. total spending or Money GDP) is the most that can be achieved by fiscal, monetary or exchange rate policy. If Money GDP can be kept on a stable path, a contribution will be made to avoiding fluctuations in output and employment as well to securing price stability. If these modest goals can be achieved, the climate may also be improved for the long-term growth of output and employment. But to go directly for stated output and employment objectives is to risk falling flat on our faces—as many politicians have discovered to their cost.

Stabilising the growth of Money GDP is itself a difficult enough objective without taking on anything more. There is the problem that estimates of Money GDP appear about $2\frac{1}{2}$ months after the end of the quarter to which they refer and are subject to considerable revision. Moreover, the quarter-to-quarter path is highly erratic even when fully known. Only trends over about a year are of significance. We will not, however, lose too much sleep over these points if our main ambition is to get the general direction right over a period of years, which is probably the most that is possible.

The two main ways in which the national authorities can influence total spending or Money GDP are government budgets and central banking policy. It is convenient to use the PSBR as a summary of fiscal (i.e. budgetary) policy and money supply (the total of notes and coin and bank deposits) as a measure of monetary (i.e. central banking) policy. Both these magni-

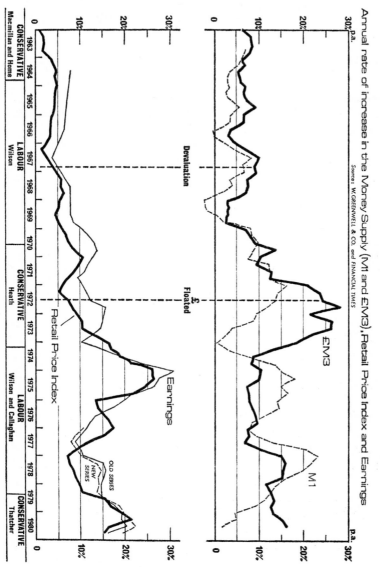

CHART 6

Annual rate of increase in the Money Supply (M1 and £M3), Retail Price Index and Earnings

Source: W.GREENWELL & CO. and FINANCIAL TIMES

Devaluation

£ Floated

£M3

M1

Earnings

Retail Price Index

OLD SERIES

NEW SERIES

| 1963 | 1964 | 1965 | 1966 | 1967 | 1968 | 1969 | 1970 | 1971 | 1972 | 1973 | 1974 | 1975 | 1976 | 1977 | 1978 | 1979 | 1980 |

| CONSERVATIVE Macmillan and Home | LABOUR Wilson | CONSERVATIVE Heath | LABOUR Wilson and Callaghan | CONSERVATIVE Thatcher |

tudes can be defined in many different ways and there is nothing sacrosanct about a particular definition.[1]

The money supply and the PSBR are termed intermediate targets since—if the argument of this *Paper* is correct—they are useful mainly as a means of influencing Money GDP, which is the final objective. (Two different measures of the money supply and their relationship to prices and wages are shown in Chart 6.)

It is worth having targets or guidelines for intermediate variables based on the best available view of their relation to money GDP. In view of the enormous influence of wishful thinking and interest-group pressures, and the political desirability of limiting the discretionary powers of our rulers, it is also worth insisting on these guidelines with a certain obstinacy and not adjusting them with every passing inconvenience or fashionable new econometric finding.

But, just as it is wrong to be carried away by over-ambition and to conduct the whole discussion in terms of 'real' objectives which governments cannot determine, it is equally mistaken to become too technocratic and to think only of the intermediate objectives. In the last resort, the money GDP objective should be the overriding one; and there should be no cries of 'blown off course' or 'U-turn' if changes in the specification of intermediate objectives prove necessary, i.e. *really* necessary and not merely convenient.

Central banking

Individuals and corporate bodies have a reservoir of spending power ranging from real things such as bricks and mortar or machinery to token claims such as shares, bonds, bank deposits, notes and coins. The more easily these forms of wealth can be used to pay for goods or services or to settle debts, or can be transformed into such means of payment, the nearer they are to money. These distinctions are matters of degree. Cattle, coins, shells, cigarettes and other weird and wonderful objects have been used as money and could be again in the absence of superior alternatives.

Central banks can influence the creation of liquid assets by

[1] Some economists prefer to analyse fiscal policy in terms of the direct injection or withdrawal of spending power in the Budget. Others prefer to think in terms of assets issued to the private sector to finance the PSBR and their effects on financial wealth.

the private sector, and thereby total spending or Money GDP. Lord Kaldor is right to draw attention to the difference between commodity currency, such as gold coins or notes convertible into gold, and paper credit.[1] In the first case the supply of currency is physically limited. In the second people can create as much money as they feel prudent by issuing IOUs to each other. Which particular IOUs will be used to settle debts will vary a great deal; and there is no hard-and-fast dividing line between money and non-money.

Nor, however, is the distinction between commodity and credit systems clear-cut. Even when gold and silver coins were the predominant form of currency, there were bank deposits, bills of exchange, IOUs of prominent traders, and many other instruments which were accepted in payment of debt and were to all intents and purposes money, even though they were not 'backed' by more than a fractional reserve of gold or silver.

In either system the central bank has an influence. Institutions such as commercial banks whose IOUs are likely to be presented for payment have to have a reserve of other bits of paper—known as banknotes—which their customers will accept. With a pure gold standard such notes will be convertible into precious metals by the central bank on demand. Why under our present system bits of paper bearing a picture of the monarch should be regarded as more genuinely cash than a receipt from, say, the National Westminster Bank is not clear. It is probably a hangover from the period when official banknotes *were* convertible into gold; and, though cynics may scoff, the association with government may also enhance their acceptability.

Deposits with the central bank (e.g. the Bank of England) have the quality of being convertible into national banknotes. Thus these deposits constitute a key part of the reserves of the commercial banks. Financial institutions such as building societies, which do not enjoy the 'privilege' of holding central bank deposits, have reserves in the shape of deposits with banks which do; they also hold short-term IOUs easily convertible into cash.

A central bank can influence monetary conditions by varying the amount of reserves the commercial banks hold with it. It can do so directly by buying securities from or selling securities

[1] Treasury and Civil Service Committee, *Memoranda on Monetary Policy, op. cit.*

to them ('open-market operations'), or by extending or withdrawing credit.

Bankers' deposits with the central bank are sometimes known as 'base money'. Under a 'monetary base system' the central bank would have a target for 'base money' which it would enforce by open-market operations.[1] If the proportion of 'base money' to total deposits can either be estimated in advance or is laid down by order, the total of bank deposits, which are the most important demand in the money supply (notes and coins being the remainder), is subject to official control. Alternatively, under the traditional system the central bank stands ready to offer unlimited credit to the banks if they require extra reserves, but at a penalty price[2] (known as 'bank rate', 'minimum lending rate' or, in some countries including the USA, the 'official discount rate'). The central bank then operates by influencing interest rates. The higher interest rates go, the less bank credit will be demanded and therefore the smaller the amount of deposits that will be created. The central bank's task is then to guess the level of interest rates consistent with its monetary target.

Central bankers prefer an interest rate policy since it increases their own discretion and makes the whole process more mysterious. But, contrary to a common misconception, either method of operation allows them to act as 'lender of last resort'. If they are consciously controlling the quantity of bank reserves, i.e., the monetary base, they must be prepared to allow the interest rate they charge to rise or fall to whatever level will choke off or stimulate demand for reserves to the required extent.

The consequent volatility in short-term interest rates is almost certainly worth accepting if it helps to stabilise the wider economy. But monetary base control is not black magic. There is no reason to expect the ratio of commercial bank deposits to reserves (the 'base multiplier') to be at all rigid and a mandatory ratio can be easily by-passed. Indeed, rigidity

---

[1] Strictly speaking, bankers' deposits and notes and coins in their tills are known as the 'narrow base'. Most economists who advocate control of the monetary base have in mind a 'wide base', which includes also notes and coins in the hands of the public. But it is still true that bankers' deposits with the central bank are the part of the base most directly affected by open-market operations.

[2] In the UK it has done so indirectly by lending to the discount houses which have then been able to repay loans to the banks; but the principle is the same.

would be curious in a market system that responds to prices and interest rates.[1] During the Great Depression when the US money stock dropped by 30 per cent and velocity fell by another 30 per cent, the monetary base was well maintained.

Thus the idea of a constant, steady growth target, or a gradually declining one, which has existed in the UK for the money supply itself, would probably be quite unsuitable for the monetary base. The latter would require a series of short-term targets, for a few months at a time, which might jump about quite a lot depending on official estimates of bankers' demand for reserve holdings.

In periods of extreme crisis or panic, like the early 1930s in the USA, it might not be sufficient simply to flood the banks with reserve assets (in the jargon, 'supplying them with base') in the hope that they would lend and thereby create sufficient deposits. It would be sensible on such occasions for the government to borrow directly from the banks to finance some of its own spending. This would avoid the need to 'push on a string' (a metaphor for the difficulty of extending bank credit to the private sector when the demand for it is limited, even at very low interest rates).

The above argument shows why the monetary targets should be set for the money supply itself, and why base control, if it is used, should be merely a mechanism. The operation of monetary targets is, in any event, full of pitfalls, especially if there is any element of half-heartedness or 'unbelieving monetarism' among those in charge.

One celebrated method of cheating is known as 'base drift'. The name has nothing to do with the monetary base, but describes the practice of making each year's monetary target a percentage of the total money stock as it stood at the end of the previous year. Thus past over-shooting is built into each new short-term target and the quantity of money rises further and further above that consistent with any medium-term anti-inflationary strategy.

There is a fascinating section in the 1981 Report of President Carter's outgoing Council of Economic Advisers[2] which shows how the low monetary targets for the five years 1976-80 coincided with high rates of growth of nominal GDP. The demand for money shifted downwards—or, in other words, velocity rose more than expected. In addition, the targets were

---

[1] Niehans, *op. cit.*, Chapter 3.   [2] *Op. cit.*, p. 52.

CHART 7

THE HIERARCHY OF OBJECTIVES

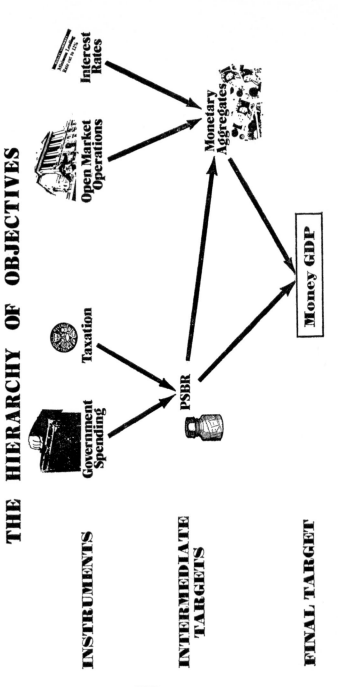

INSTRUMENTS

INTERMEDIATE TARGETS

FINAL TARGET

exceeded in three years out of the five. The biggest increases in velocity took place in the two years 1976 and 1979 when the official monetary target was hit.

Budget deficits

The idea that governments should balance their budgets and forget the complications will certainly have occurred to some readers. But it has no clear meaning, even if we leave 1930s-type crises out of account. Mr Gladstone's Budget was small and simple enough, and sufficiently undistorted by inflation or nationalised industries to be treated as a single current account to be financed from revenue. Today there is no one right way of measuring the balance.

Do today's budget balancers want to eliminate the whole PSBR, which amounted to £13·5 billion in 1980-81, or the Financial Deficit, which excludes some lending operations and transactions in securities and came to £11·8 billion? Do they want to exclude the nationalised industries, thus reducing the Deficit to £8·8 billion?

Some people argue that even the Financial Deficit is not genuine since, in 1980-81, for example, some £7·7 billion of it was used for expenditure classified as capital, leaving a current shortfall of only £1·1 billion.[1] The objection to this argument is that most government capital spending produces no ascertainable revenue and a social return which can only be guessed; it is thus not really comparable with the kind of spending which commercial enterprises will reasonably finance by borrowing.

Such questions could be posed indefinitely. If the public sector accounts are presented on an inflation-adjusted basis, the PSBR disappears completely in many recent years (Table IV). The main reason for the adjustment is that inflation reduces the value of the National Debt and enriches the public sector. (A similar effect occurs in inflation-adjusted corporate accounts when a company is regarded as gaining from the erosion in the real burden of its fixed interest debt, a process known as the 'gearing adjustment'). The paradoxical result is that the government's accounts look healthier in years of high inflation and rising nominal interest rates, such as 1976, when the real value of the National Debt falls most heavily. For in

[1] *Financial Statement and Budget Report* ('Red Book') *1981-82*, HMSO, 1981.

[67]

TABLE IV

INFLATION-ADJUSTED PUBLIC SECTOR
BORROWING REQUIREMENT, 1968-71 TO 1980
Adjustments by Bank of England

	1968-71	*1972-75*	*Annual averages* *1976*	*1977*	*1978*	*1979*	*1980*
Nominal PSBR (£bn)	0·6	5·8	9·1	6·0	8·3	12·6	12·3
'Real' PSBR* (£bn)	−2·0	−1·7	0·6	−3·5	1·5	−1·5	−2·6

*This line is arrived at by subtracting from the nominal PSBR the amount by which the National Debt is reduced in real terms by inflation.

Source: Third Report from the Treasury and Civil Service Committee, Session 1980-81, *Monetary Policy*, Vol. I: *Report*, HC163-I, HMSO, 1981, p. xcix.

these years the government enjoys the maximum legalised default on its borrowings.

There is thus no alternative to estimating, by a mixture of trial and error and analysis of data for the past, a trend path for the PSBR likely to be associated with the desired growth of Nominal GDP. It can be done either directly or by relating the PSBR to the desired growth of some monetary aggregate (as shown in Chart 7). The final target, it must be repeated, is Money GDP. It is then a fine question whether to have two sets of intermediate targets—one for the PSBR and one for the money supply—or intermediate targets for the monetary supply alone, with the PSBR adjusted *ambulando*.

Inflation renders all numbers or percentages relating to budget deficits and public sector borrowing virtually meaningless over a long time-span—much more so than in the case of the money supply. Suppose we were told that the PSBR in Britain would be £20 billion in the year 2000. It might be enormous or chicken-feed depending on how much £20 billion is worth that year. If the PSBR was to be expressed as a proportion of the national product, say 10 per cent, we might hazard a guess that the policy stance would be inflationary. But it could be from a starting point where the general price level was half

TABLE V

PUBLIC SECTOR BORROWING AND INFLATION: INTERNATIONAL COMPARISON, 1977-79

Country and item	1977-79 annual average
	%
United States	
Public sector surplus or deficit (—) as per cent of GNP[1]	−0·1
Inflation rate	8·4
Germany:	
Public sector surplus or deficit (—) as per cent of GNP[1]	−2·7
Inflation rate	3·5
Japan:	
Public sector surplus or deficit (—) as per cent of GNP[1]	−4·8
Inflation rate	5·1

[1] Standardised national accounts basis.

Source: US Council of Economic Advisers, *Report to the President, 1981, op. cit.*

the present one, twice as high, or ten, a thousand, or a billion times higher.

The more immediate case for according a subordinate rôle to fiscal targets is illustrated by Table V, which shows how variable is the relationship between public sector borrowing and inflation. Such tables do not demonstrate the irrelevance of the PSBR, as foolish polemicists assert, but merely that its size consistent with monetary stability varies from country to country and period to period.

Adjusted balance*

The case for pursuing a target PSBR over a whole economic cycle rather than in particular years is well known. When private (or international) saving is buoyant or investment depressed, the government can borrow more without over-heating the economy or driving unemployment below its sustainable rate (or CIR).

The theory of the 'constant employment' budget suggests that the target PSBR should be set for a normal trend year when employment and activity are neither unsustainably high nor exceptionally low. The revenue-reducing and expenditure-boosting effects of a recession which enlarge the budget deficit would then be regarded as permissible and, indeed, desirable. The less popular corollary is that the PSBR should be below target (or a budget surplus should be achieved) in times of boom.

Of course, the strength of the built-in stabilisers will depend on characteristics of the fiscal system, such as the ratio of social security benefits to normal pay, which have been designed for ends having nothing to do with macro-economic stability. If economists are clever enough to work out that the permissible budgetary overshoot in a recession should be 75 or 150 per cent of what occurs automatically, then by all means let us try to devise schemes for securing this result. It is, of course, untrue to suppose that the bigger the automatic effect the better. If lags are long, too large a correction could actually aggravate instability.[1]

By far the biggest practical difficulty is to estimate what sustainable level of unemployment (CIR) is to be used to provide the benchmark for the correction. The temptation to over-optimism has already been noted. In the formulation of a medium-term budgetary path it is wise, except in the most extreme cases, to start from the existing state of affairs and accept only overshoots and shortfalls which are due to *future* variations in activity.

Even then the process of cyclical correction is fraught with nightmares. The British Treasury worries a great deal because the revenue that will be gained when the economy moves out of recession will vary widely according to the composition of recovery—whether it is predominantly exports, stocks, invest-ment, home consumption or government spending. Much more important than this copybook problem is uncertainty over the extent to which the financing of heavy deficits in the national-ised industries and of 'lame duck' rescues should be counted as policy decisions or as automatic responses to recession.

Monetary targets*

Why should there be a presumption in favour of a stable growth of the quantity of money while the PSBR can be allowed to

---

[1] Milton Friedman analyses the issue in *Essays in Positive Economics*, University of Chicago Press, Chicago, 1953.

vary with the cycle? One reason is the evidence that the effects of monetary policy are subject to longer lags than fiscal measures. A large rise in the monetary aggregates is liable to trigger off a powerful delayed-action effect on Nominal GDP and hence inflation, the most notorious, but not the only, example being the Heath monetary explosion of 1971-73.

The attractions of a money supply rule go even further. The enormous uncertainty about (a) what the target PSBR should be over a cycle, and (b) how much 'automatic' over-shoot or undershoot should be allowed in individual years, were noted in the previous sub-section. It would be a great convenience if monetary targets and techniques could be evolved which provided an automatic check on the appropriate-ness of the fiscal guidelines.

An example of how monetary guidelines can provide some guidance on how far to adjust budgetary targets occurred during the turmoil following the oil price explosions of 1973-74 and 1979-80. Both oil crises brought with them a major up-surge in the desire to save out of income in the newly-enriched oil-producing countries. It surely made sense then for oil-consuming countries to run larger budget deficits—financed by borrowing the extra OPEC savings—while adhering to monetary targets as a fail-safe device against overdoing matters and setting off runaway inflation.

A successful régime of monetary targets thus provides a powerful check on fiscal behaviour. For, if the rate of public sector borrowing leads over the years to either accelerating monetary growth or accelerating interest rates to prevent that happening, it is a sign that the fiscal targets have been wrongly set. But if the underlying fiscal target is right, stabilising forces come into operation. In a recession, when borrowing is de-pressed, it should be easier than in a normal or boom year to finance a larger budget deficit without pressure on interest rates. Thus an appropriate monetary rule will provide some guidance for fiscal stabilisation as well.

Unfortunately, this harmony between a cyclically adjusted PSBR target and money supply guidelines will not always be present. Recessions do not always follow the same pattern. The UK recession which began in 1980 was unusual in the extent to which it was initiated by severe pressure on profit margins resulting from a rising real exchange rate. The consequence was a much larger amount of distress borrowing in the early stages than in any previous recession. To finance a recession-induced PSBR overshoot on such an occasion while holding to the monetary target may involve a rise in real interest rates hardly appropriate to a depressed economy. Indeed, despite a serious breach of the monetary targets, real interest rates did rise in the UK to quite high levels in the winter of 1980-81. The Treasury Committee Report discussed the idea of cyclical variations in monetary as well as PSBR objectives, but then drew back.[1] It argued that if cyclical adjustments were made to both the PSBR and the money supply, the credibility of a 'Medium-Term Financial Strategy' would be undermined.

The occurrence of such conflicts between fiscal and monetary objectives underlines the importance of subordinating these intermediate objectives to an overriding strategy in terms of Money GDP or total spending, which should be the key variable in explaining policy developments to the public. There is all the difference in the world between a sincere scrutiny of instruments and definitions to aid policy and a cynical search for whatever definition of money or of the PSBR seems to have grown least.

Overseas demand for sterling

One of the most important complications in monitoring the monetary aggregates is the need to get away from 'monetarism in one country'. As a matter of logic, inflation or deflation can occur because of a change either in the supply of money or in the demand for it. Traditional monetary theory, with its emphasis on a single country and currency, has located inflationary and deflationary disturbances on the supply side. In today's world it is an excessive simplification. The trade-weighted exchange rate of sterling rose by about 30 per cent from the middle of 1977 to the end of 1980—a period during which UK costs increased faster than those of its main competitors. The money supply in the UK also rose faster than in other main trading countries, even though the UK's output trend was considerably lower.

Part of the reason for sterling's appreciation was North Sea oil, which displaced oil imports and allowed the UK to balance its current account with a smaller volume of manufacturing

---

[1] Third Report from the Treasury and Civil Service Committee, Session 1980-81: *Monetary Policy*, Vol. I: *Report*, HC163-I, HMSO, 1981, para. 6.25 to 6.31.

exports relatively to imports. But the direct terms of trade effect of North Sea oil (accounting for a sterling appreciation of perhaps 10 per cent) was not nearly large enough to explain the whole of the pound's rise in world currency markets.

Riding on the back of North Sea output like an elephant on a camel was a much larger flow-of-funds effect. The combination of large OPEC surpluses, political and financial uncertainties about Germany and the USA, and political stability and assured energy supplies in Britain was making the UK a magnet for footloose international funds. These factors boosted the direct impact of North Sea output several-fold.

Despite agreements to 'phase out' its rôle as a reserve currency, the amount of sterling held by overseas national authorities rose by £1·4 billion in the four years to the end of 1980 to reach £4 billion. Sterling liabilities to non-official overseas holders rose by £6·5 billion to reach £10 billion, easily a record. Moreover, the *ex post* figures do not tell the whole story. The pound had to rise to balance the increasing demand for sterling with the available supply. At an unchanged sterling rate the build-up of overseas balances would have been even higher.

These shifts in overseas demand explain why sterling rose and inflation fell much faster than expected in 1979-80, despite the overshoot in the domestic money supply.[1] The combination of North Sea oil and huge footloose OPEC surpluses led to an increase in the demand for sterling even bigger than the increase in supply.[2]

---

[1] That overseas holdings of sterling are excluded from all official definitions of the money supply was irrelevant to the economic forces at work.

[2] There is another possible domestic explanation related to 'overshooting'· Suppose that British inflation has in the past always been 5 per cent per annum faster than the rest of the world's and nominal interest rates 5 per cent higher, and that sterling is consequently expected to depreciate by 5 per cent each year. Suppose some event occurs, such as the announcement and introduction of a more stringent financial strategy, which causes markets to believe that British inflation will now be the same as the world average and that there will be no further long-term depreciation in the exchange rate. As a result of this event the one-year forward exchange rate for sterling rises by 5 per cent. If nominal interest rates are initially unchanged, an American holder of funds in London would experience an increase in his expected dollar return of 5 per cent. The rush of funds to London to take advantage of this profitable opportunity (an example of 'arbitrage') would drive the spot exchange rate for sterling *up* by 5 per cent *immediately* to eliminate this excess profit. Thus the exchange rate does not merely stop depreciating but initially appreciates or 'overshoots' by 5 per cent

[*Contd. on p. 74*]

As always when demand exceeds supply, the price rose. A rise in the price of sterling in terms of marks or dollars meant that German or American goods were much cheaper to buy with pounds than before. This exerted pressure on profit margins and made the recession in the UK worse than elsewhere. At the same time it induced British producers to hold down their costs and prices to stay alive in the international market. The result was a drop in the inflation rate exceeding all forecasts, and a drive to reduce costs and improve efficiency of a severity which no British government committed to gradualism would have dared to attempt consciously.[1]

Companies were squeezed between the large wage increases of 1979-80, following the collapse of the Callaghan incomes policy, and the exchange rate appreciation which prevented them from passing on the higher wages in higher prices. Faced with intense pressure on profit margins, companies were forced to borrow large amounts. In the 12 months from the starting point of the monetary target in February 1980, sterling M3 rose by 20 per cent—twice the target range of 7 to 11 per cent a year. The overshoot could have been stopped only by draconian increases in interest rates and widespread bankruptcies. The newly-created money was largely paid out to employees and ended up mainly in the personal sector where it lay dormant (i.e. velocity fell), partly because growing job insecurity in-

---

[*Contd. from p. 73*]

before drifting back to its new equilibrium. If domestic interest rates have to be raised temporarily as part of the new policy, the overshooting is bigger still.

This explanation of sterling's rise, and the one in the text in terms of a shift in international portfolio demand, can both be true. But the portfolio diversification story has the advantage not only of laying less weight on British government policy announcements but also of fitting in better with the timing of events. The 1979-80 rise in the trade-weighted sterling exchange rate began early in 1979 with the disruption of oil supplies from Iran following the deposition of the Shah. This was well before even the announcement of the May 1979 election, let alone its result.

[1] When in 1978 the Swiss National Bank was confronted with strong overseas demand for Swiss francs, it suspended its monetary targets and intervened vigorously in the market to buy foreign exchange, in effect creating new francs to meet the external demand. Because of its long-established reputation for monetary rectitude, the Swiss central bank seemed to get away with this departure from past practice in the sense that it did not adversely affect expectations about the domestic price level. The public believed that the change was temporary and not a shift to inflationary policies. The basis of this confidence was, of course, Switzerland's experience with near-stable prices over many years. It was not so easy to recommend that the Bank of England should respond to overseas demand for sterling by gaily creating even more.

CHART 8

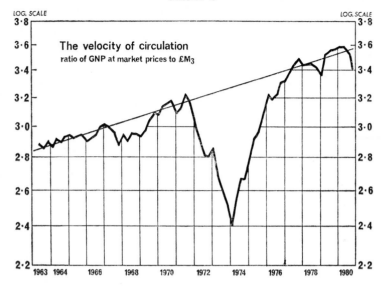

creased people's desire to save and hold liquid funds. A contributory factor was the abnormally high level of short-term interest rates in relation to long-term ones. The resulting distortion of the yield curve encouraged people to hold an unusually large fraction of their financial assets in the form of deposit accounts at banks.

If the effects of the 'corset' removal had been foreseen, the 1980-81 target for sterling M3 might have been set at around 11 to 15 per cent. Even then the growth which did occur would have been a serious overshoot. The excess did not matter in that year because of the rise in both overseas and domestic demand for sterling for holding purposes. The latter was reflected statistically in the fall in the velocity of circulation. But past experience (illustrated in Chart 8) casts doubt on the permanence of this fall. More likely than not, idle UK balances would become active once the worst of the recession was over.

The 1981 Budget and 'Red Book' were deliberately ambiguous about whether any of the excess money created in the past year would be clawed back. Nevertheless, that much-denounced Budget did try to bring the PSBR under control, while making some allowance for the recession. This gave the Medium-Term Strategy a further chance to fight for existence, but in an increasingly hostile environment of know-nothing inflationist critics.

UK medium-term strategy

In retrospect it is easy to see that the original sterling M3 target for 1980-81 was too tight, even from the point of view of those who were happy with the speed at which inflation declined. The 7 to 11 per cent a year target range was first instituted by the new Conservative Government in June 1979 through the simple process of reducing by 1 per cent the Labour Government's target of 8 to 12 per cent for the year to April 1979. That target had actually been met. The incoming Conservative Government's target of an annual 7 to 11 per cent increase was also met in the 10 months to April 1980, for which it originally ran before being extended one more year.

The Bank of England bears some responsibility for providing misleading intelligence. When Sir Geoffrey Howe became Chancellor of the Exchequer in May 1979 a scheme known as the 'corset' was in operation (for the third time since December 1973). Its correct name was the Supplementary Special Deposits Scheme. This placed a ceiling on the growth of interest-bearing deposits for every bank. Offenders were required to make penal deposits with the Bank of England on a heavily rising scale.

The 'corset' was essentially a cosmetic device; for it led to the diversion of transactions to forms where they would not create additional bank deposits and thus escape the 'corset' penalties, the clearest example being the substitution of bills for overdrafts. It thus made the official money supply figures misleading, similar to the way that a tampering with the mercury makes a thermometer misleading.

Unfortunately the Bank persuaded Sir Geoffrey against removing the 'corset' on his arrival in office. As a result, the target of 7 to 11 per cent appeared both less restrictive and easier to achieve than proved to be the case when this artificial device was at last removed in June 1980. The Bank then underestimated the effects of the removal of the corset and, to add insult to injury, cheerfully allowed Treasury Ministers and officials to take the blame. Not only that: having first tried to kill the Medium-Term Financial Strategy, the Bank did much behind the scenes to incite criticism of the Government's supposed obsession with sterling M3.

[76]

The most sensible recommendation for a country such as the UK is to base its monetary targets on long-term trends in the relationship of money GDP to the domestic monetary aggregates, rather than on individual freak years. That in occasional years inflation may as a result be reduced faster than expected is probably an advantage, given the original starting point.

The fail-safe device to prevent such rule-of-thumb guidelines from exerting an excessive deflationary pressure is to keep a weather eye directly on money GDP. How far should money GDP be merely monitored and how far should an attempt be made to forecast it and regulate policy to prevent a dip before it occurs? It is a question of art, judgement and instinct. However strongly rules and guidelines are entrenched, individuals will always have to interpret them. Any plan for the finances of a nation or company must contain a delicate balance of continuity and flexibility. This truism is not a reason for jettisoning all statements of intention or for leaving everything to the discretion of those immediately in charge of operations.

APPENDIX TO IV

*Money and Credit**

Much blood has been spilt over the difference between money and bank credit and the appropriateness of rival measures of both for official target purposes. Much unnecessary mystification has thereby been produced.

Money is primarily a medium of exchange. But it is also a unit of account in which contracts are expressed and values are stated. The money used for the two purposes can be different. In medieval commercial centres there was often a 'money of account' for expressing contracts different from the great variety of gold and silver coins of varying weight and purity in which payments were actually made. In modern times a divergence of this kind is a sign of currency breakdown, since it is normally convenient to make the unit of account the same as the medium of exchange. Money has a third function as a store of wealth in which it competes with many other assets.

Today money consists largely of bank deposits and, to a smaller extent, notes and coin. These are all bank liabilities (notes and coin being the liabilities of the central bank). Different measures of money include different groups of liabilities. To each measure of money there is a corresponding 'credit' measure on the assets side.

[77]

TABLE VI

THE BANKING SECTOR'S BALANCE SHEET

Liabilities:
  Sterling deposits:
    UK residents
    Overseas sector
  Foreign currency deposits
  Non-deposit liabilities (net)

Assets:
  Sterling lending to:
    UK public sector
    UK private sector
    Overseas sector
  Foreign currency assets

The relationship is illustrated in Table VI. Liability, or 'money', measures will be slightly less than credit ones by an amount corresponding to the net non-deposit liabilities of the banks, mainly shareholders' capital.

A monetarist, in the strict sense, will focus on the money or liabilities side. He will do so because he believes there is a systematic relationship between money and a few key variables, above all income, but also expected inflation, interest rates and (in some models) total financial wealth. The transmission mechanism is from money to these other variables; thus if the amount of money is changed the other variables will shift until the normal relationship is restored. But even to a strict monetarist, bank credit is important as a mechanism by which money comes into existence. There is thus no reason to be up in arms if statistics or targets are presented in terms of the assets (or credit) side of the banking balance sheet.

For other schools of thought credit is important as a source of spending (for investment or consumption purposes) over and above expenditure out of current income. Bank credit, whether advanced to the government or the private sector, is simply one very important source of credit but does not differ in principle from other kinds such as trade credit, or lending on debentures, which do not give rise to a monetary counterpart. There is, of course, no reason why bank credit should not be important for both its money-creating and its investment-financing aspects. But our concern here is primarily with the monetary aspects.

All official definitions of the money supply exclude sterling deposits held by overseas residents, now about an eighth of the total (although, as has been seen, overseas purchase of sterling assets of any kind can have a profound effect on the price level and on economic conditions in the UK). The official definitions also exclude non-residents' foreign currency deposits held in London. These are more than twice as large as all sterling deposits. Dollar deposits in London are supposed to have little inflationary or deflationary influence on the UK economy and are no different

TABLE VII

THE DIFFERENT MEASURES OF MONEY SUPPLY

	£million, mid-May 1980 *(not seasonally adjusted)*
1. Notes and coin in circulation with public	9,706
UK private sector sterling sight deposits:	
2. (i) Non-interest bearing	14,271
3. (ii) Interest bearing	3,601
4. M1 ($=1+2+3$)	27,578
5. UK private sector sterling time deposits	29,065
6. UK public sector sterling deposits	1,210
7. Sterling M3 ($=$M1$+5+6$)	57,853
8. UK residents' deposits in other currencies	6,248
9. M3 ($=£$M3$+8$)	64,101

Source: Treasury Progress Report, July 1980.

in principle from dollar deposits in Zurich or Singapore, except for the invisible earnings they bring to UK banks.

The banking liabilities which go into the varying definitions of money are listed in Table VII. The main distinction is between 'broad money' (sterling M3), which includes deposit accounts, and 'narrow money' (M1), which excludes them. The Bank of England plans to publish an intermediate measure, M2, which would exclude so-called wholesale deposits (such as Certificates of Deposit), regarded as nearer to a pure investment than to a means of payment.

Still wider measures of 'private sector liquidity' are now published by the Bank of England. PSL1 includes, in addition to bank deposits, 'other market instruments' of which very much the most important are deposits with local authorities and certificates of tax deposit. PSL2 consists of PSL1 plus savings deposits. Deposits with the National Savings and Trustee Savings Banks are, for instance, included, but overwhelmingly the most important extra ingredient is 'shares and deposits with building societies'. (The Treasury Committee *Report on Monetary Policy* wrongly stated they were excluded (p. cxiii).) Many of these instruments are quite near to ordinary bank deposits in their functions, and scrutiny of the wider aggregates is an important check on the money supply measures when the

TABLE VIII

MONEY SUPPLY GROWTH AND ITS COUNTERPARTS

£million, 1979-80
(not seasonally adjusted)

	PSBR	9,795
less	Net acquisition of public sector debt by UK non-bank private sector	–9,110
plus	Increase in sterling bank lending to:	
	(i) UK private sector	9,336
	(ii) overseas sector	489
equals	DCE	10,510
less	Increase in external and foreign currency finance	–2,644
less	Increase in banks' net non-deposit liabilities	–1,417
equals	Increase in sterling M3	6,449

Source: Treasury Progress Report, July 1980.

latter are distorted by statistical complications, policy changes or market imperfections.

The main officially-monitored credit measure, Domestic Credit Expansion (DCE), is (approximately) the sum of bank lending in sterling to the public, private and overseas sectors (Table VIII). (Overseas lending to the UK government by overseas governments and banks is also included in DCE, more for moral than for accounting reasons as the definition was invented by the IMF to monitor countries in overseas payments difficulties.)

Under a flexible exchange rate system, DCE and the growth of sterling M3 are similar. But under a fixed exchange rate they can move far apart. In general, DCE is greater than the growth of the money supply when there is a deficit on the overall balance of payments (current plus capital account) and smaller than the growth of the money supply when there is a surplus. A DCE target thus leads to a tightening of monetary policy when there is a payments deficit and a loosening when there is a surplus. It is thus appropriate to a fixed exchange rate régime, while a money supply target is more appropriate to a floating rate régime when overseas payments balance automatically and the government and central bank are free to pursue domestic objectives.

If the reader feels that all these definitions are rather arbitrary and correspond to no hard-and-fast distinctions in real life, he is right. The most appropriate measure to control is that which gives the closest fit with Money GDP. If the monetary variable chosen for an intermediate target moves in a very different way to other monetary measures we should be suspicious, since it will often mean that people have found a way of using assets for monetary purposes which are just outside the official definitions.

V. MONEY IN LONGER-TERM PERSPECTIVE

Historical stability misleading

It will not have escaped the reader's attention that this *Paper* suggests regulation of the quantity of money as a technique of demand management. Although the government and central bank should try to keep their intermediate targets as stable as possible, those should still be subordinate to the broader targets for Money GDP.

This prescription is undoubtedly different in spirit from the automatic-sounding Friedman rule of a fixed annual growth of the quantity of money based on the indisputable historical association between monetary changes and price movements. The problem is that we have almost no experience of price stability arising from man-made control of a purely paper or fiat currency inconvertible into a particular commodity.

> '[The] fundamental objection to the adequacy of the pure quantity theory of money is that, even with a single currency in circulation within a territory, there is, strictly speaking, no such thing as *the* quantity of money, and that any attempt to delimit certain groups of the media of exchange expressed in terms of a single unit as if they were homogeneous or perfect substitutes is misleading . . .'

This is a quotation from Professor F. A. Hayek[1] but could equally have come from the Radcliffe Report of 1959, notorious for its downgrading of monetary policy. The mistake made by Radcliffe, but not by Hayek, was to suppose that, because money was difficult to measure, the limitation of its supply was unimportant.

Historically, periods of price stability have been those in which the monetary unit consisted of precious metals (stamped into convenient units of standard weight known as coins) or of IOUs, notes or bank deposits convertible into specie. Superficial rationalists have rebelled against the idea of the amount of money being determined by anything as arbitrary as the supply of certain metals. But it was never as arbitrary as that.

---

[1] F. A. Hayek, *Denationalisation of Money—The Argument Refined*, Hobart Paper 70, IEA, 2nd Edn., 1978, p. 77.

When the money stock threatened to be inadequate the real value of gold and silver rose, creating an incentive to develop banking and credit facilities and to economise on bullion supplies. Columbus set out in search of gold and silver at a time of deflationary pressure, when the commercial revival of the 15th century was being hampered by insufficient supplies of those metals.

For the purpose of examining a period when there was no conscious policy of controlling the quantity of money, the exact definition of money does not matter. The amount of money was determined by the gold or silver base and by the credit pyramid erected by competitive banking institutions. Official policy was concerned at most with the convertibility, and not with the size, of bank deposits. Individuals decided whether to hold cash, current ('checking') bank accounts or deposit ('savings') accounts. These might be subject to different long-term velocity trends; but it makes little difference whether the historian claims that a rate of growth of 2 per cent in narrow money or 3 per cent in broad money was consistent with price stability. Slightly different monetary rules can be formulated retrospectively; but overwhelmingly the most important principle seems to be that monetary growth should be kept at a modest rate. A wrong definition would seem to lead merely to slowly creeping inflation, easily correctable by a modest downward adjustment of the monetary target.

Similarly, the problem of whether to monitor money, financial assets or even total wealth did not arise. There was no large deadweight government debt (i.e. debt not backed by productive assets), and financial assets might be expected to grow roughly in line with the nation's real wealth multiplied by the price level. Any tendency to flood the market with bond issues would have been corrected by a debasement of their value relatively to that of money and real things, and a consequent increase in their yield. Currency, financial and real assets would grow in rough proportion to the nation's wealth in periods of stability; and prolonged inflationary or deflationary episodes would reveal themselves whatever asset was used for measuring purposes.

Currency substitution

Historical experience is not necessarily a good guide to the behaviour of a purely token system when one particular range of financial assets classified as 'money' is being controlled. Experience of price stability on this basis is mainly confined to a few South East Asian and Central European countries in the 1970s. The achievements of the latter now look distinctly shaky, and in any case offer too small a body of empirical evidence from which to generalise.

The defects of monetarism, in the narrow sense of the fixed rule for domestic money supply, are that it concedes too much power to official intervention, underrates the influence of competition in providing monetary substitutes, and takes official statistics far too much at their face value. 'Friedmanites' are often very good at analysing how controls and regulations in the economy generally will be avoided or will produce unintended effects quite different from those their sponsors desire. But too often they evince a touching faith in government in their own special sphere.

The invention of new monetary instruments to replace old ones—and competition between currencies—is becoming more important as communications improve further and capital markets become even more closely linked. The abolition of exchange control in Britain in 1979 was bound to create complications for the measurement and control of the quantity of money, as the evolution of the Eurodollar market (defined below, note to page 85) had already done for the USA.

It is upside-down logic to suggest it was therefore wrong to abolish exchange control or reduce barriers between capital markets. The reluctance of people to hold a freely-tradable worldwide currency which depreciates rapidly and erratically is a bigger long-run constraint on inflationary policies than monetary targets achieved by controls and manipulations which distort the meaning of the aggregates controlled.

Monetary challenge and response

There have been two main types of response to these challenges from those central banks which have been seriously interested in preventing the over-issue of their currencies. At one extreme there has been the attempt to tighten up control methods to stop leakages—exemplified by the US Federal Reserve Board ('the Fed'). Not only does the Fed monitor several definitions of money; it has also adjusted the definition of the measure ('M1B') of its principal monetary target. The old definition, known as M1, was of currency plus current accounts (in US parlance, 'checking' or 'sight' accounts). It had become inadequate because techniques had developed, such as Negotiable Orders of Deposit (referred to as 'Now' accounts), which enabled deposit accounts ('savings' accounts) to be used for making current payments. The new M1B includes these Now accounts.

The Fed has tried to plug other leaks by extending its jurisdiction to non-member banks. Under the Depository Institutions Deregulation and Monetary Control Act of 1981, non-member banks must submit periodic reports to the Fed and also begin to hold deposits with it. The Fed has also tried to persuade overseas central banks to impose reserve requirements on the dollar operations of non-American banks, so far without success.

At the other extreme, the Swiss National Bank has adjusted its operating techniques to the practices of financial markets. It imposes no official reserve requirements on the commercial banks. They choose freely the ratio of their deposits with the National Bank to their total deposits. The National Bank engages in open-market operations—in practice, foreign currency purchases from and sales to the banks—on the basis of its own estimates of the ratio of total deposits to reserves which the banks will want to hold.

The two approaches are not mutually exclusive. It is possible to have fairly tight controls à la Fed but also to make the legal requirements correspond as closely as possible with what the banks would want to do on the basis of commercial prudence.

When banks are prevented from expanding at home by reserve asset requirements in excess of their own prudential limits, they will expand overseas where such restrictions do not apply. This is the most fundamental explanation I have seen of the evolution of Eurodollars and other Euro-currencies.[1]

Of total Euro-currency deposits estimated at 1,100 billion dollars in 1980, the greater part was accounted for by interbank deposits, that is, transfers from one bank to another. Some 200 to 250 billion dollars represented deposits by, or lending to, the non-bank public. Part of this amount was already included in national estimates of the quantity of money, leaving about

---

[1] Eurodollars are deposits in non-American banks denominated in dollars. They arise, for instance, when an American transfers his dollar deposit to a foreign bank, but keeps it in dollars. 'Euro' versions now exist of most prominent currencies.

150 billion dollars of stateless money not appearing in any country's monetary totals. Such deposits are estimated to have grown by an annual average of 25 per cent in the decade to 1980, compared to a growth of 15 per cent in the broadly-defined monetary aggregates of the main industrial countries. Even so, stateless deposits of Euro-currencies held by the non-bank public still amounted to only about 6 per cent of the banking assets of the main industrial countries.[1]

Thus the growth of Euro-currencies has not yet become a major threat to control by central banks over the world's money supply. But it *could* become so and is in any case illustrative of the leakages in methods of monetary control which operate against the self-interest of existing or potential financial institutions.

The most effective approach is to make mandatory and prudential reserve requirements correspond more closely. Then there will be less incentive to invent new financial instruments (such as money market mutual funds in the USA) outside the existing definitions of money or outside the scope of central bank regulations. It may also help if the incentive to avoid mandatory reserve requirements is reduced by paying market-related interest rates on deposits with central banks, and for the income of the latter to be derived from some other source than the non-payment of interest on commercial banks' deposits.

Such attempts to work with, rather than against, the market will help to plug unnecessary leakages in monetary control. But they are not in the last resort intellectually satisfying. If people wish to issue more IOUs to each other and use them for making payments, they will eventually find a way. Central bank efforts to stop this are likely to result mainly in the transfer of activities from New York, Frankfurt or London to the more exotic financial centres outside their effective jurisdiction. The real charge against central banks is not that they have failed to stop private individuals or institutions from creating monetary assets; it is that they have added to the supply of these assets on their own initiative, either to finance their governments' activities or in pursuit of their own policy objectives, ranging from interest-rate targets to the rescue of insolvent private sector institutions.

---

[1] Morgan Guaranty, *World Financial Markets*, December 1980; David Lomax, *National Westminster Bank International Supplement*, 9 June 1980.

Among those who are daunted by the problem of controlling state paper currencies, by far the most popular proposal is to go back to a gold standard. Money has in practice more often been based on silver than on gold. It was the 19th-century silver discoveries, which depressed the free market silver-to-gold ratio well beyond the traditional 15/16 to 1, that spelt the end of silver as a monetary standard. The lesser metal is still priced far below its old level in relation to gold.

With a pure gold standard, money consists of gold coins ('specie') or of notes backed one hundred per cent by gold. Under a fractional gold standard other kinds of money exist with only a fractional gold cover. There is no hard-and-fast dividing line between the two types; they form a continuous spectrum. In 1689, outstanding means of payment consisted of about £210 million in specie and £10 million in bank notes, deposits, bills of exchange and other media. By 1914, £145 million in specie were outweighed by £45 million in bank notes and £1,075 million in bank deposits—the latter, of course, being convertible into bank notes which were in turn convertible by the Bank of England into gold.[1] The most attenuated form of gold exchange standard was the post-war Bretton Woods régime. Currencies were convertible into dollars which in turn the US Treasury would convert into gold—but only for *bona fide* monetary authorities, not for US citizens. In the last few years of gold convertibility before it was suspended by President Nixon in 1971, conversion even for monetary authorities was undertaken only with the greatest reluctance.

The US authorities always denied that gold convertibility had any effect on their internal monetary policies, which, if true, explains why the system collapsed. What is certain is that the Fed did not pursue a conscious money supply policy, but rather an interest rate one which by fortunate coincidence led for a while to fairly stable monetary behaviour. When the Vietnam War and the budget deficits of the late 1960s rendered conventional interest rates incompatible with stable US monetary growth, the whole post-war monetary order exploded.

Many who talk of going back to the gold standard mean no more than a return to the Bretton Woods system of 'gold parities' for currencies, which would be used to determine

[1] T. Congdon, 'The First Principles of Central Banking', *The Banker*, April 1981.

exchange rates but would not make national money convertible into gold for private holders. Gold movements would take place only to settle payments imbalances between national authorities.

Even to maintain such a gold exchange standard a new official price would have to be fixed for gold—which, in view of recent market movements, would have to be between 10 and 30 times the 35 dollars per fine ounce level of 1971. People could hardly fail to notice that all currencies had been devalued against gold to this extent, and it would therefore be nonsense to talk of an immutable standard such as prevailed in the UK for two-and-a-half centuries before 1914.

Everybody would know that a major devaluation of all currencies against gold had happened very recently and could happen again. Since such a vestigial gold standard would operate like a Bretton Woods exchange-rate 'peg', it would at most be only a moderate inhibition on a government inflating above the world rate. Devaluation would be available as a not-so-last resort.

In the more radical form of the gold standard proposal, domestic currencies would also be convertible into gold on demand for private holders. This would impose a stronger constraint on inflation. But it would still come up against the lack of incentive for governments to maintain convertibility at a pre-ordained rate when the going became rough. The original gold standard depended on the belief that money was not merely convertible into gold or silver but in fact *consisted* of those precious metals, for which on occasion IOUs might be created. It depended on the myth that catastrophe would occur if a country 'went off gold'; and a myth by its nature cannot be artificially re-created.

But the most fundamental difficulty would arise from the desire to economise on stocks of precious metals. As in the 19th century, it would lead to multiple reserve banking, i.e. the creation of large deposits on a small reserve base known as 'pyramiding'. Everything would depend on whether there were built-in incentives to prudence on the part of financial institutions with considerable money-creating power.

Competitive money

The disadvantages and lack of credibility of a new gold standard lead us to consider Professor Hayek's proposal for free competition between currencies, so that Gresham's Law can be reversed and good money drive out bad. Hayek has made two proposals. The first is for the free circulation of existing national currencies across the exchanges. This, of course, is already possible in countries without exchange control, which include the USA, the UK and Germany. Why then do not people already switch to good currencies when their own are seen to be subject to risks of depreciation? Taxation may be part of the reason. The UK owner of an investment in an alternative currency which had maintained its real value and appreciated by, say, 10 per cent against sterling would be taxed as if he had made a capital gain. The whole tangle of tax and accounting complications relating to the revaluation of corporate overseas assets when exchange rates change would invade national business transactions as well.

Many of the advantages of alternative currencies for unit-of-account purposes could be obtained through contracts linked to a general price index or expressed in a stable foreign currency, even if the medium of exchange remained the domestic currency. Yet such contracts seem to become widespread only when strato-inflation has persisted for a long period, as in Latin America. People will pay a high price to stay with a familiar unit of account.

The second, and more far-reaching, form of Hayek's proposal would allow the introduction of private enterprise currencies, not necessarily related to an official unit. The proposal takes us into uncharted territory. There is no widely accepted theory of the results of free competition between privately-issued currencies. During periods in the past when different currencies circulated side by side they were nearly always gold and silver coins of varying weight and purity.

Modern experience in frontier countries has been of competition between official currencies. There is hardly any experience of competition between true private enterprise token currencies; it is highly likely that any successful private enterprise currencies of the future will turn out to be commodity-based.

Gold is not the best candidate for a commodity-based currency. In the USA, a commodity basket containing 33 cents worth of ammonium nitrate, 12 cents worth of copper, 36 cents worth of aluminium and 19 cents worth of plywood (all at 1967 prices) has moved in close relation to the US cost-of-living index since World War II, performing in this respect far better than gold.[1]

'Unbelieving monetarists'

Price stability in the very long run probably depends on the simultaneous fulfilment of two conditions:

(a) the availability of commodity-based currencies; and

(b) free choice between alternative means of payment and standards of value to allow the reverse of Gresham's Law to hold and provide a deterrent to undue pyramiding on the commodity base.

It would be a characteristic 'rationalist fallacy' to try to lay down a blueprint for fulfilling these conditions. All we can do at present is to minimise the obstacles put in their way by unwise policies. Rather than speculate further about the currency of the future, it is more rewarding to return to the evidence of the past. The record shows that, despite all the banking crashes, financial bubbles and other crises resulting from the exuberance of unrestrained profit-seeking, the great and persistent historical inflations originated in the financing of government.

The main exception is the 16th-century discovery of precious metals in the New World, which was the result of the profit-seeking quest for gold and silver. Even then the inflation rate averaged less than 2 per cent a year—very slow and creeping by the standards both of the currency debasements engineered by monarchs and of 20th-century experience.

As for more modern times, it is difficult to think of any post-gold standard example of runaway inflation or deflation due mainly to technical monetary control difficulties. In almost all instances governmental authorities failed to control money supply because either:

(a) they gave priority to attempts to spend their economies into full employment; or

(b) they were unwilling to allow nominal interest rates to rise in the short term, often as a result of political pre-occupation with home loans; or

(c) they gave priority to exchange-rate objectives (usually a special case of (a)).

[1] Robert E. Hall, *Explorations in the Gold Standard and Related Policies*, National Bureau of Economic Research, Washington DC, 1981.

[90]

VI. JOBS AND PAY

Asking the right questions

Economists who see inflation in terms of monetary demand have been pursued by politicians with the question: 'How much unemployment will it take and for how long to reduce inflation by x per cent?' (or, '. . . to eliminate it altogether?'). Since programmes to reduce inflation have a transitional cost—even if they are better handled than in Britain in 1979-80—it is a legitimate question.

When unemployment appears to be above its long-term trend, another question is equally legitimate: 'How much extra inflation will we have and for how long if we try to reduce unemployment by x?'.

The second inquiry is the mirror image of the first. It is the way in which the issue most often arose in the USA in the 1960s and 1970s. And it is the way in which it could arise in Britain in the 1980s.

It was suggested earlier that no general answer to such questions can be read off a set of equations because so much depends on the state of expectations, beliefs about policy, and the confidence with which the beliefs are held—as well as on unpredictable but quite frequent shocks which can knock the economy off course. Politicians will have to live with these uncertainties or resort to the many charlatans who will offer confident answers.

But not only are inquiries about the temporary trade-off between unemployment and inflation difficult to answer; they are also superficial and of little help to the formulation of employment policy. The key question for employment policy is: 'What is the rate at which unemployment will settle after inflation has fallen to the target level and various shocks, whether induced by policy or not, have worked their way out of the system?'. In the terminology of this *Paper*: 'What is the minimum sustainable rate of unemployment?'. (I have called this rate the CIR or MIR; it has been promulgated by Friedman under the unfortunate name of the 'natural rate'.)

Although it is difficult to estimate this rate precisely, it has certainly risen steeply since the early 1960s. The MIR is closely related to the average or trend rate over a number of years, but it is not quite identical. An upward trend of inflation is *prima facie* evidence that unemployment is being held *below* its sustainable rate. Falling inflation is evidence that unemployment is *above* its sustainable minimum. With a fixed exchange rate, inflationary pressures are diverted to the balance of payments and the MIR will be equivalent to the average unemployment rate only if overseas payments remain in balance without recourse to official overseas borrowing or the loss of reserves.

Between 1952 and 1964, UK adult unemployment averaged beteeen 300,000 and 350,000—or less than 1½ per cent—and inflation was creeping along at about 3 per cent a year with little discernible long-term trend. For most of the time there was a small surplus on the overseas current account and a balance on total official financing. But a marked tendency towards an overseas payments deficit developed in the early 1960s; it became substantial in the middle of the decade and culminated in the 1967 devaluation.

In the following decade the floating of the pound more or less eliminated the balance-of-payments distortions. Inflation rose in a series of large irregular swings to double-digit percentage rates, reaching a peak (year-on-year) of 24 per cent in 1975 and a subsidiary peak of 18 per cent in 1980. Unemployment grew in each successive cycle, reaching 850,000 in the 1971-72 recession, 1·4 million in 1977, and hardly dropping below 1·3 million at the cyclical peak of 1979. In the spring of 1981 it stood at 2½ million (or just over 10 per cent, with a denominator made up of the total employees plus registered unemployed of 24·1 million). Official predictions were that it would level off at 2·7 to 2·8 million in 1982-83 (excluding school-leavers and allowing for seasonal fluctuations).

Steadily rising equilibrium rate of unemployment

These data seem consistent with Professor Patrick Minford's estimate of an equilibrium (or MIR) unemployment rate rising from 1½ per cent in the early 1960s to 2½ per cent in the late 1960s, 6 per cent in the late 1970s, and 8 to 8½ per cent— or about 2 million—in the early 1980s.[1] This last estimate is

---

[1] *The Economic Outlook*, Liverpool Occasional Papers, No. 1, 1981.

CHART 9

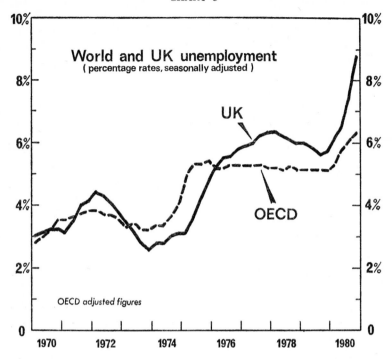

World and UK unemployment
(percentage rates, seasonally adjusted)

of where unemployment will settle once official policy is no longer concerned with reducing inflation and economic agents have adapted to the prevailing monetary and fiscal framework and to the prevailing exchange rate.

An alternative estimate has been provided by the Treasury. It has stated that, on the basis of its equations for wages and prices, the unemployment rate at which inflation might be expected to remain stable is about 5 per cent, or 1·2 million.[1] The estimate probably contained an element of playing safe; and the Treasury expressed scepticism about its own equations. The true MIR is almost certainly nearer the Minford figure (which itself was received as wildly optimistic by economists who rejected the MIR concept altogether and who expected unemployment to go on rising indefinitely without a major government stimulus).

This trend rise in unemployment has taken place under

[1] *Fifth Report from the Treasury and Civil Service Committee,* Session 1980-81, HC 232-II, 9 April 1981, p. 27.

governments of all persuasions and has been worldwide, although it has recently been worse in the UK, as Chart 9 demonstrates. Why has it occurred? Those who argue that the level of employment is not in the long run determined by demand management have an obligation to offer an alternative explanation of the forces at work, even if they cannot provide a conclusive answer.

The British economy has had to adjust itself not only to

(a) an exceptionally rapid reduction of inflation from the 1980 peak (which I have described as a transitional effect) but also to

(b) the effect of North Sea oil in crowding out non-oil exports;

(c) the long-delayed attack on overmanning which was precipitated by the sharp rise in the real exchange rate in 1979-80 and consequent pressure on profit margins;

(d) the sharp increase in energy prices which has made many processes and products obsolescent;

(e) the drift in the most efficient location of many traditional manufacturing industries to the newly industrialising countries.

The last two are common to other industrial countries, the first three unique to Britain. They have combined to produce a very heavy manpower fall in manufacturing industry.

The meaning of unemployment

But before going in a little more detail into these forces and the obstacles which have prevented the workers released from finding employment elsewhere, it is worth analysing more closely the nature of unemployment. Statistics of unemployment can be studied in two ways, in terms of stocks and in terms of flows.

The stock concept is the most popular and is represented by the total of registered unemployed published each month. The notion of a stagnant pool of jobless people is, however, extremely misleading. Every month large numbers of people both enter and leave the unemployment register. The number leaving the register, mostly for new jobs, has varied very little over the last two decades within a range of 250,000 to 300,000; this was so even during the sharp rise in unemployment that took place in the winter of 1980-81. Many people go straight into new jobs without registering as unemployed; and the total number of engagements is estimated by the Manpower Services Commission (MSC) to be over 7 million a year.[1]

The growth in unemployment in 1980 resulted from an increase in the number of people joining the register; from a position of approximate equality with those leaving, it rose to a rate of around 360,000 a month at the end of 1980. Although the *stock* of outstanding vacancies fell by about 60 per cent between the autumn of 1979 and the end of 1980, the reduction in the *flow* of notified vacancies was only some 30 per cent. The discrepancy was, of course, accounted for by the speeding up of the rate at which vacancies were filled.

To examine unemployment in terms of flows is in no way to belittle the problem. Indeed, the number of people registering as unemployed in the course of a year is much larger than the 'stock' figures of the monthly totals; in 1980 it amounted to about 4 million (though this sum is an over-estimate since some individuals register more than once in the course of a year).

In the mid-1960s, around half the people who became unemployed left the register within a fortnight, which was thus the median[2] length of time out of work. By the mid-1970s the median had risen to about a month. There are no up-to-date estimates for the winter of 1980-81 but the best guess is that it had risen to about three or four months.[3]

High unemployment makes itself felt for most of those affected in a longer interval between jobs, with associated uncertainties and anxieties. But the number of long-term unemployed (the stagnant pool element) increases too. Because many of the people who are going to be unemployed for more than a year have only just entered the register at the onset of recession, the number in that category is understated in the monthly count. Although the number of unemployed registered for more than a year was 400,000 in January 1981, according to MSC calculations previous trends implied a rise in the total in that category to about 600,000 in 1983, even without much further deterioration in the jobs market.

---

[1] Manpower Services Commission, *Manpower Review, 1981*, HMSO.

[2] The median represents the middle position in any group where there are equal numbers above and below that position.

[3] W. Daniel, 'Why is High Unemployment Still Somehow Accepted?', *New Society*, 19 March 1981.

It is well known that the stock figures of unemployment in the monthly count overstate the total in some ways and understate it in others; and large bodies of literature are devoted to proving that one or the other distortion predominates. The MSC has estimated unregistered unemployment at about 350,000.[1] On the other side, rather more than 200,000 of the unemployed are classified by employment offices as 'having poor prospects and being unenthusiastic about work'. There are also about 100,000 occupational pensioners below the age of 65 registered as unemployed, although some of these have very low pensions. The two opposing schools can carry on indefinitely seeking items to add or subtract in a stale, weary and unprofitable controversy.

Most of the attempted statistical adjustments tell us only a small part of what we really want to know. There is little information about 'discouraged' workers who left the labour force because of the state of the job market and no longer say they are looking for work. The purported statistical corrections also leave out fraudulent unemployment, whether of the utterly bogus variety or where there is a failure to declare modest earnings on the side.[2]

The search for the 'true' unemployment rate is a vain pursuit since no hard-and-fast dividing line exists between 'voluntary' and 'involuntary' unemployment in the world in which we live. Many people who do not regard themselves as part of the labour force at all could be enticed into employment if offered sufficiently attractive and well-paid work. Equally, a number of the unemployed could doubtless find work if they were prepared to accept a sufficient drop in pay or change in conditions. The word 'unemployable' should never be used by market economists. Rather they should ask: 'Employable at what price?'; and, if they have a social conscience: 'How could they become employable on better terms?'.

The price of labour

However we choose to measure or evaluate it, an unemployment problem emerged in the 1970s and has increased in the early 1980s. Why has this happened?

[1] Manpower Services Commission, *Labour Market Quarterly Report*, HMSO, February 1981.

[2] According to the Rayner Report on unemployment benefit, a minimum of 8 per cent of all claims are fraudulent (*Payment of Benefits to Unemployed People*, HMSO, 1981).

The clue to an answer is that the quantity of labour of different kinds demanded and supplied depends, like any other service, on the costs and prices in the relevant markets.

The demand for labour depends on the real wage, seen as a cost by the employer, i.e. wages (including employers' social security contributions) as a proportion of value added—or, as it is sometimes called, the 'product wage'. If the cost of labour of given productivity is increased, less of it will be bought. This, incidentally, has nothing to do with 'capitalism'. It applies to state socialism and to the market in direct services where people engage craftsmen, plumbers, gardeners and others to do jobs without the intervention of an employer or other intermediary.

The demand for labour depends not merely on the average level of real wages but also on the pattern of *relative* wages for different skills, occupations, industries and areas. Even if the average pay level is appropriate, people can still be priced out of work if relative wages are not at market-clearing levels. In this case unemployment in some areas is likely to coincide with labour shortage in others. The two types of distortion aggravate each other since the shortages hold down total output and thus reduce the demand for workers in the areas of labour surplus.

Being priced out of work is not necessarily the consequence of aggressive union pressure for higher real pay. It may result from passive resistance to *downward* shifts in the market-clearing real wage, either in the whole economy or in particular sectors.[1]

The supply of labour depends not only on the number of people of working age and on social habits but also on the cost of not having a registered job. The latter is determined by such factors as benefit levels, work expenses and tax thresholds, as well as by the value of, and opportunities for, 'unofficial' work,

---

[1] According to one interpretation of Keynes's *General Theory*, workers *cannot* lower their real wages because, if they tried to, employers would reduce prices, either in competition with each other or by retaining a conventional mark-up. This certainly does not apply to the export and import-competing sectors in the UK or other European countries where prices are at least partially set in world markets. The point of Keynes's observation was to suggest that, in a 1930s-type situation, monetary demand should be increased rather than money wages reduced. Then final prices would rise and the real product wage fall. But if, as has been the case in most post-war cycles, wages rise in response to higher monetary demand, it must mean that workers choose not to accept the real wage reduction on offer.

whether perfectly legal 'do-it-yourself' activities or unregistered jobs in the 'black economy'.

To say that real wages have diverged from market-clearing wages is a statement of the problem, not an answer. The important issue is *why* they have diverged.

'Money illusion'

There is no shortage of plausible explanations for the trend rise in unemployment; on the contrary, a wealth of suggestions has been offered. The difficulty is to discriminate between them and give each of them its appropriate weight.

One explanation relies on the alleged persistence of *money illusion* for a large part of the 1950s and early 1960s. In that period people accepted that a pound was a pound and a dollar was a dollar, and took little account of the slow upward creep in prices of about 3 per cent a year. In other words, they accepted lower wages than they could have obtained in the prevailing state of the labour market, which enabled the economy to be run at a level of unemployment lower than was possible after money illusion was punctured. In terms of Chart 2 (page 38), the economy was at point P where unemployment was below its true equilibrium.

Looked at in the historical perspective of Chart 10, both the very high unemployment rates of the 1930s and the very low post-war ones seem abnormal, and a return to something in between should not be all that surprising. My own view is that the puncturing of money illusion may explain some of the unemployment deterioration between the two post-war decades and the 1967-73 period. But it is doubtful whether it explains the severe further deterioration since then.

An alternative explanation of the recent period—in terms of inflation—works the other way round. It claims that, whatever the effect of 3 per cent creeping inflation, the *high and fluctuating inflation of between 6 and 25 per cent* which the UK has experienced since 1970 itself contributes to severe unemployment for the reasons explained in Section III. On this analysis, the long-term cure for unemployment is to reduce inflation as much as possible.

I have no doubt that high and uncertain rates of inflation have aggravated unemployment. But there is no evidence to suggest either that they are the only or even the predominant factor or that with low inflation unemployment would return

CHART 10

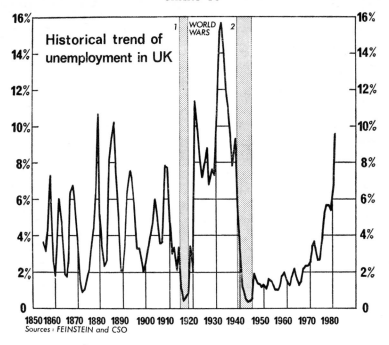

Historical trend of unemployment in UK

Sources : FEINSTEIN and CSO

to a satisfactory level (even if we beg all questions and regard 4 to 4½ per cent, or around 1 million unemployed, as satisfactory). Indeed, the emergence of anxiety about unemployment in a low-inflation country such as Germany (where labour market changes are dampened by the movement of 'guest workers') suggests that other forces are at work as well.[1]

A further explanation, which often appeals to people who emphasise inflationary upheaval, is *political instability*. The adversary winner-takes-all political system, with its notorious U-turns between and during Parliaments, has not provided a stable framework for business planning. In particular, it has engendered the fear that a government would come to power which did not accept the legitimacy of the profit motive or the mixed economy. An economic system might be able to function with many different types of property rights, including collectivist

---

[1] Mrs Thatcher and her Ministers sometimes speak as if it followed from the denial of the proposition that *carrying out* inflationary policies would reduce unemployment that *refraining from* inflationary policies would reduce it. The two propositions are contraries, not contradictories, and they can both be false together.

ones. But an uncertain definition or enforcement of these rights, together with the absence of widely-accepted norms of legitimate political action, makes rational business planning exceedingly difficult.

Again, I have no doubt that electoral reform, which would remove from the business community the bogey of a 'Benn Government', would help investment and employment. But the upward trend of unemployment in countries without these particular British problems renders the explanation less than conclusive. The emergence of a Social Democrat-Liberal group holding the political balance may make it possible to introduce some reforms, such as the revival of a market in rented property, which would, by promoting mobility, lower the sustainable unemployment rate. But that is a different matter from ascribing the whole of the trend on the right of Chart 10 to the post-war battle between the two main political parties.

Structural changes

There have clearly been important structural changes since the 1960s which have affected the demand for various categories of workers. The oil price explosion itself made a good deal of existing equipment obsolete, thereby reducing the ratio of usable capital to labour. Published surveys of spare capacity do not take adequate account of this obsolescence.

The development of North Sea oil production to the point of self-sufficiency (achieved in 1980) was bound to change the structure of demand for labour. The reason follows from the fact that the current account on overseas payments must balance, except to the extent that there are net exports or imports of capital. The country has become wealthier as a result of the oil and now needs to export fewer non-oil products to pay for the imports required to support a given volume of activity. It is because manufactures constitute a higher proportion of exportable goods than of final sales in general that they bear the brunt of the re-adjustment. The famous Kay-Forsyth article estimated a 9 per cent fall in manufacturing output—not absolutely, but *compared* with what it would otherwise have been—as a result of North Sea oil, but an 8 per cent increase in private services, construction, housing and public administration.[1] The authors assumed a constant level of real activity

[1] P. J. Forsyth and J. A. Kay, 'The Economic Implications of North Sea Oil', *Fiscal Studies*, July 1980.

and no attempt to shift resources away from the public sector. But to the extent that these structural changes are resisted, real activity falls and the favourable shifts fail to materialise.

The impact of North Sea oil is, however, only part of a broader structural shift away from manufacturing affecting most of the advanced countries. A major element lies in the take-off which occurred in the 1970s in the growth of the so-called Newly Industrialising Countries (NICs). In the last decade, the developing world taken as a whole did not share the developed countries' experience of falling growth; indeed, it maintained a considerably higher rate of expansion.

Economic growth tends in its early stages to be predominantly in the manufacturing sector. When a group of hitherto under-developed countries embarks on a process of rapid growth the result is likely to be an addition to the world supply of manu-factured goods, far larger than the addition to primary product or service output. The price of manufactured goods will tend therefore to fall, in a free market, relatively to other goods and services. The developed countries are still large producers of manufactures, but have costs of production (measured at equil-ibrium exchange rates) far higher than the NICs for at least the main standard products. They have thus been the main sufferers from the deterioration in the terms of trade of pro-ducers of manufactures.[1]

Faced with a deterioration in the real prices it can obtain for manufactures (or in sales prospects if prices are held up against market pressures), business in the developed countries has found it in its interest to shift from manufacturing to other sectors of activity. Tentative evidence in support of this hypothesis is provided by the data on profitability rates in different UK sectors (Table IX).

The severity of the structural shift can be demonstrated by comparing the last two recessions. The total fall in real GDP from the 1973 peak to the 1975 trough is estimated by the Central Statistical Office (CSO) at just under 4 per cent. The fall in GDP from the 1979 peak to the two quarters spanning the end of 1980 and the beginning of 1981 is estimated at nearly 6 per cent. But, for manufacturing, the decline in output was very much larger—just over 9 per cent in the earlier recession and nearly 19 per cent in the recent one (in this

[1] Michael Beenstock and P. Willcocks, 'The Causes of Slower Growth in the World Economy', London Business School (mimeo), 1980.

TABLE IX

SHARES OF PROFIT* AND INVESTMENT IN NET OUTPUT

Measured by value added

	1951-55	1956-60	1961-66	1967-73	1974-78
Percentages					
Profits/value added					
Manufacturing	34·9	32·1	29·8	27·1	20·2
'Private services'	38·7	39·8	35·4	36·4	36·1
Investment/ value added					
Manufacturing	15·4	15·5	15·7	14·6	15·0
'Private services'	5·5	7·4	9·9	11·7	12·2

*Including depreciation, but excluding stock appreciation.

Source: Maurice Scott, *The Unemployment Policy Discussion in the UK*, Nuffield College, Oxford.

respect only, inviting comparison with the inter-war depression).

Unemployment enters the picture *via* the 'mismatch hypothesis' which states that, when a major structural shift is taking place, resources will not flow instantly from the old unprofitable sectors into the new ones with growth potential; during the transition total output will be depressed. Of course, to speak of manufacturing *versus* service activities is itself an oversimplification. There will be trends within manufacturing from old-fashioned 'heavy' industries, such as steel and cars, to electronic software and other activities which are much more skill-intensive and are likely to remain profitable in the older developed countries, as are speciality products of all kinds.

The mismatch, or structural change, hypothesis explains many otherwise puzzling features of current unemployment, such as the coincidence of labour shortages in some areas and job shortages in others, and long delivery delays for some products with surplus capacity for others. The 1981 MSC *Manpower Review* expresses the fear that skill shortages will re-emerge in the next upturn even when general unemployment is in the 2 to 3 million range.

The mismatch hypothesis also helps to explain the rôle of producer groups and perverse government policies. For the older entrenched industries tend to be both more heavily trade union-dominated and more politically influential than the new growing sectors. Thus both union and political power can be expected to be heavily mobilised when the older sectors are threatened with decline.

Another factor peculiar to Britain has been the intensive attack on overmanning which began with the 1980 recession or just before. It was triggered off by the intense pressure on profits resulting from the high real exchange rate already discussed. The effect was, however, to concentrate into a very short period changes which had been postponed for years or even decades.

In view of all these adjustments, even with a well-functioning labour market there would probably have been several years of relatively high unemployment while the required shifts of resources were taking place. To preserve full employment in the face of these shifts, wage costs in many sectors would have had to fall as a proportion of value added. In fact, they rose nearly everywhere. Labour costs (wages and salaries and employers' National Insurance contributions) moved in a way likely, other things being equal, to price people out of work (Table X). Income from employment grew from an average of 75 per cent of total costs in 1959-69 to a peak of 82½ per cent in 1975. It then fell back to 78 per cent after the early phases of the Callaghan-Healey pay policies, but shot up again in 1979-80 in the explosion which normally follows the collapse of such policies. Similar information has already been cited in Table IX from the point of view of gross profits—what is left of value added when labour costs are subtracted. There is a striking contrast between the fall in profit as a proportion of value added in manufacturing and its maintenance in private services, at least up to the recent recession; this difference has been reflected in the investment and employment behaviour of the two sectors.

The way in which high real wages price workers out of jobs is more subtle than Ministerial rhetoric suggests. It takes a good deal of time for the real wage effects to have their full impact. There is always scope for more or fewer people in, for example,

TABLE X

OUTPUT COSTS, 1959-69 TO 1980

Composition of net domestic product at factor cost[1]

Percentage

	1959-69[2]	1970	1971	1972	1973	1974	1975	1976	1977	1978	1979	1980
Factor incomes after providing for stock appreciation and capital consumption												
Income from self-employment	8·4	8·6	9·2	9·9	10·7	9·6	8·6	8·7	8·7	9·0	9·2	9·4
Net trading profits and rent of companies	12·2	9·4	10·0	10·2	9·9	4·7	4·7	5·4	7·6	7·9	6·6	5·1
Net trading surplus and rent of public corporations	1·0	0·6	0·3	0·4	0·5	0·1	−0·1	0·7	0·8	0·5	−0·1	−0·3

Net trading surplus and rent of general government	1·2	1·5	1·4	1·1	1·1	1·1	1·3	1·2	1·2	1·2	1·2	1·2	1·1
Rent income of personal sector	2·2	2·9	3·0	2·9	2·9	2·8	3·4	3·2	3·3	3·5	3·4	3·4	3·3
Net profits and other income	24·9	23·0	23·8	24·4	24·4	24·9	19·1	17·5	19·3	21·7	22·0	20·2	18·5
Wages and salaries	69·2	70·1	69·2	68·4	68·4	67·5	72·2	72·9	70·3	68·4	68·3	69·8	71·1
Employers' contributions	5·9	7·0	6·9	7·2	7·2	7·5	8·7	9·6	10·3	9·9	9·7	10·0	10·4
Income from employment	75·1	77·0	76·2	75·6	75·6	75·1	80·9	82·5	80·7	78·3	78·0	79·8	81·5
Net domestic product	100·0	100·0	100·0	100·0	100·0	100·0	100·0	100·0	100·0	100·0	100·0	100·0	100·0

[105]

[1] Net domestic product is equal to gross domestic product *less* capital consumption at current replacement cost.   [2] Annual average.

Source: Economic Trends, October 1980, p. 126, and subsequent issues.

care and maintenance. But the most important consequence of wages being too high is that chosen production techniques take on an excessively capital-using and labour-saving bias.

This can be a fairly long-drawn-out process. In some areas, ranging from retailing to gardening, methods can alter quickly in response to relative changes in labour and capital costs. But in many other areas—services as well as manufacturing—technological change is a matter of years and it takes a long time for labour to price itself into or out of work.

It is therefore wrong to look for the main effects of real wages on employment in year-to-year changes. The movement is rather from one business cycle to the next. The worrying aspect of unemployment has not been its rise in recessions but its long-term upward drift since the mid-1960s.[1]

Mrs Shirley Williams, a former Cabinet Minister, rightly points out that regional and industrial policy in many countries has often aggravated the shift towards excessively labour-saving and capital-using techniques by subsidising capital-intensive investment in regional policy grants and by taxing labour.[2] Even if all the taxes and subsidies are shifted onto the final price, there is still an artificial stimulus to capital-intensive, as distinct from labour-intensive, processes and products.

The perverse rise in the wage share is partly due to mistakes in short-term policy, such as the mishandling of the 're-entry' into normal collective bargaining after the collapse of the Labour Government's pay policies (symbolised by the Clegg awards), the mistaken shift from income tax to VAT by the incoming Conservative Government in 1979, and, above all, by the lag in the response of the two sides of industry both to

---

[1] That is probably one of the main reasons why there has been some difficulty in demonstrating the effect statistically. Here, as elsewhere, econometric studies can be cited to support almost any view. One study reported in *Lloyds Bank Economic Bulletin* for March 1981 finds little correlation between real wages and unemployment. On the other hand, J. Symons claims that employment in manufacturing responds to changes in the product wage with an elasticity of 'something less than −1, but with a lag of seven quarters before even half the effect is felt' (*The Demand for Labour in British Manufacturing*, Centre for Labour Economics, London School of Economics, 1981). The most interesting aspect is that the model breaks down for 1978, the last year of the sample period, when it greatly over-predicts employment. Phases 1 and 2 of the Healey pay policies led to a drastic reduction in the product wage. Symons suggests that firms may have sat on their hands because they did not believe that the change would be reasonably permanent, a belief borne out by events.

[2] Shirley Williams, *Politics for People*, Penguin Books, 1981; also *OECD Observer*, March 1981.

the new Government's financial strategy and to the implications for the exchange rate of sterling becoming a petro-currency. These are all transitional shocks which can aggravate a particular recession, but they are unlikely to be responsible for the adverse *long-term* trend in the jobs market. The estimates already cited of the minimum sustainable unemployment rate (MIR) are for a time when the economy has adjusted to all the short-term shocks.

To explain the perverse movement of the real wage in an upward direction inimical to full employment it is also necessary to examine influences on the side of labour supply. These include areas like housing, tax and social security, trade union activities, and so on. But simply listing distortions will not help explain a *rising* unemployment trend, which requires the distortions to have *become worse* or to have interacted with each other more than in the past.

Supply side influences

(i) *Housing*

Housing policy imposes a notorious distortion on the labour market. An unemployed steel-worker with a wife and four children occupying a council house in Durham will, quite rationally, think several times before moving to, and re-training for, a job in the south. Less often discussed are the effects of subsidies for house owners in the shape of tax relief on mortgage interest and the abolition of Schedule A.[1] Not only do they make it politically difficult to phase out the subsidisation of the rents for council dwellings and rent controls so as to treat housing as a private good; they also encourage overinvestment in a single main residence relative to other assets, which can hardly be good for mobility.

There is some evidence that housing obstacles to labour mobility have increased. The privately rented sector has traditionally housed the youngest and most mobile part of the population. The decline of this sector under the impact of rent controls gathered pace in the 1970s when one-third of privately

---

[1] 'Schedule A' was a tax on the notional annual income derived from owner occupation. It was based on the idea that a person who owns his house has a higher real income than another person with an identical money income who has to pay rent. Schedule A was based on ever-increasing under-valuation of house property and eventually abolished by Mr Selwyn Lloyd when he was Chancellor of the Exchequer in 1961.

rented units was lost. This must have been discouraging to geographical mobility, already low enough. According to the MSC estimates, only 1 per cent of the working population moves home each year for job or training purposes.

(ii) *The poverty and unemployment trap*

The social security and tax system has two potential effects on work incentives. It establishes a floor wage below which it is not worth taking a registered job.[1] But, even for people with a wage above the floor, the net gain from taking a job is reduced by the combination of lower benefit and liability to tax which constitutes the poverty trap. Both effects can lead not only to more 'search time'—that is, to people picking and choosing over a longer period to find the right new job. They can also result in more long-term unemployment if people find they have little to gain from taking the sort of job they are likely to be offered, however long they search.

An index of real social security payments, grossed up for tax (but excluding earnings-related benefits), compiled by the Liverpool Group suggests a rise of about 70 per cent in benefits over the period 1963-77 with some levelling off since then. Benefits are estimated by the Liverpool model to be about 75 per cent of the average earnings (at work) of a married man with two children whose wife is not working.[2]

In November 1980, a man with children had net spending power which varied very little whether his wage was £45 or £105 a week. His income depended more on his family circumstances, type of housing, and social security entitlements than on his earnings or, indeed, on whether he was at work or not.[3] It is not necessary to select the extreme case, where the implicit marginal tax rate from taking a job or obtaining a better one is more than 100 per cent, to see the poverty trap at work.

The subject is both highly emotive and full of technical pitfalls. The figures cited are for representative cases; individual instances differ widely. Survey evidence suggests that many of of the unemployed are much worse off than might be supposed

[1] A 'registered job' means that it is registered for income tax and National Insurance purposes. Its holder is, by definition, not in the black economy.

[2] Patrick Minford and associates, *Is the Government's Economic Strategy on Course?*, Liverpool Occasional Papers, No. 1, 1981; also in *Lloyds Bank Review*, April 1981.

[3] Ralph Howell, *Why Work?*, Conservative Political Centre, 2nd Edn., 1981.

from hypothetical calculation of benefit entitlement. The shadow economy and the benefits of do-it-yourself activity will raise the 'reservation wage' for some people some of the time, i.e. the wage below which it would not pay them to take a registered job. There is no doubt, too, that some of those workers most prone to unemployment have little opportunity for unofficial work in the black economy and suffer great hardship without a job. A rational analysis of the labour market is not a denial of social hardship and has little to do with campaigns against scroungers.

The forces affecting the poverty trap and the 'reservation wage' originate at all points on the political compass. Professor Minford has suggested that every 10 per cent rise in real social security benefits lifts unemployment by well over 2 per cent, or by about half a million. There is no need to quarrel about the direction of the effect.[1] On the other hand, an increase in the real value of child benefits reduces the poverty trap and improves the incentive to work, quite apart from its other social effects. For the higher child benefit the less the head of a family has to lose in income support on transferring from the dole to a job. This is unambiguously true up to the point where the child benefit equals the child-related unemployment benefit, which it does not at present.

One of the biggest contributors to the poverty trap has been the fall in the real tax threshold. In 1955 a head of household with two children paid income tax if he was on average earnings or above. In 1965 he started paying tax at 72 per cent of average earnings, and in 1975 at 44 per cent. By 1981 the threshold was down to 38 per cent, the problem having been aggravated by the failure of the Conservative Government in its 1981 Budget to index the personal allowances so as to avoid an increase in the basic rate of income tax, which had become a political sacred cow.[2]

---

[1] The Liverpool estimates of the effect of benefit on unemployment are higher than those suggested by the earlier work of Professor S. J. Nickell of the LSE because (a) the Liverpool estimate of the ratio of net benefit to net employment income ('the replacement ratio') is arrived at differently and shows a more prolonged upward movement, and (b) the Liverpool calculations of the impact of a given change, particularly on the long-term unemployed, are larger (S. J. Nickell, 'The Effect of Unemployment and Related Benefits on the Duration of Unemployment', *Economic Journal*, March 1979).

[2] C. Pond and C. Playford, *Carried Across the Threshold*, Low Pay Report No. 5 Low Pay Research Unit, 1981.

Raising personal allowances is, however, a very expensive way of shielding the lowest paid from income tax, since the benefit goes right up the income scale and is obviously largest for higher-rate taxpayers. There is much to be said for Frank Field's suggestion of a switch from personal allowances to exempting from tax altogether all incomes below a given amount (say, £3,000 for a married man).[1] This was, in fact, the pre-1920 system. To prevent sudden steep rises in the marginal rate, the exemption would have to taper off rather than end abruptly.

As important as the quantitative changes have been those in public attitudes. If the behaviour of students (who now do not appear in the official unemployment figures) is anything to go by, living on benefit is losing a degree of its stigma. But some remains. There are millions of people at work who would probably be as well off exploiting the social security system and earning a little in the 'unofficial' economy. If some 'desire to work' of a non-pecuniary kind did not exist it would be difficult to explain why so many low-paid people bother to seek jobs.

(iii) *Labour monopoly power*

Except for a passing reference, and to show that there are many other forces at work, I have deliberately left trade union power and other factors making for labour monopoly or interference in labour markets to the end of this incomplete list of possible causes of rising unemployment.

All these forces become much more important because of their interaction. Housing rigidities matter more when there are structural changes taking place to the disadvantage of older industrial centres. 'Why work?' symptoms matter more when available work is distant and unfamiliar. Union monopoly power is activated in order to resist downward pressures on the equilibrium wage resulting from structural changes. The interaction of these forces makes recessions deeper and recoveries shallower. But boosting demand would be of little use since the supply bottlenecks now appear at a much earlier stage of recovery than previously.

Whatever other evils are attributable to union monopolies, they are largely guiltless of the most common charge of causing

---

[1] Frank Field, *Inequality in Britain*, Fontana, 1981, p. 203.

continuing inflation. Of course, if the government imposes a squeeze on the growth of its total spending, or MV, the more unions retard the downward adjustment of wage settlements, the higher will be prices and the lower output and employment. This is a purely transitional effect. Indeed, if union power was the dominant force behind continuous inflation, it would suggest that union leaders were interested in money wages—i.e. numbers on pieces of paper—rather than real wages. They are not so irrational.

The belief that monopoly of any kind, whether enterprise or union, causes continuing inflation is based on a confusion between *higher* prices and *rising* prices, and between the *general price level* and the *relative prices* of particular commodities. If there is a monopoly in, say, soap powder, this product will be more expensive and other products cheaper (because consumers have less to spend on them) than under competition. Even if the soap powder firm has only just acquired its monopoly and raised its price yesterday, and if the prices of other goods are slow to fall in compensation ('downward price rigidities'), there is at most a knock-on effect on the price index. Inflation, by contrast, is a *continuing* rise in the general price level, year after year.

Nevertheless, although union monopoly power does not lead directly to inflation, it can cause a good deal of damage. If wages and prices are higher in the strongly unionised sectors than in the weaker and non-unionised ones, workers can be crowded into these sectors and confronted with the choice between inferior or fringe employment and living on social security.

Union pressures have priced people out of work not only in particular industries but in particular categories. One of the worst examples is their insistence that young people be paid the full adult wage irrespective of productive performance. An OECD report[1] attributed the low level of youth unemployment in Germany compared with other countries not only to the apprenticeship system but to the fact that wage levels of new entrants are adjusted to their productive capacity. Denmark has a German-type apprenticeship system, but the rate of youth unemployment there soars suddenly at the age of 18 when a minimum wage corresponding to two-thirds of average manual earnings becomes obligatory.

[1] 'Youth Unemployment', *OECD Observer*, HMSO, March 1981.

Unemployment will worsen if either union power increases or unions make more use of their existing power. The former influence can be established easily enough from the growth in union membership. According to official figures, the number of union members in the UK grew from 10·5 million in 1969 to 13·5 million in 1979, representing an increase from 45·4 to 56 per cent of total employees. Much of the growth was in the public sector which had a unionisation rate of 83·1 per cent in 1974 compared with 66·4 in 1968.[1] By contrast, the increase in the private sector over the same period was only from 33·8 to 34·8 per cent. This supports the general impression that union monopoly power is in large part a public sector problem where it is a reaction to the existence of a monopoly or semi-monopoly employer which cannot go bankrupt.

Incomes policy

Estimates of the wage distortion caused by union monopoly are very hazardous. But, for what it is worth, it has been suggested in the USA that strong unions can raise wages by up to 25 per cent above the competitive level, a more typical differential being 10 per cent. Estimates for the British differential vary between 12 and 25 per cent. According to the Liverpool model, this itself raises unemployment by up to 3 per cent, or by 750,000.

It would be too mechanistic to measure the union effect only by the percentage of workers unionised. The extent to which union monopoly power is applied depends on prevailing norms of behaviour as well as on market calculations. The electricity supply workers, for instance, clearly do not use their full power to extract higher wages and raise electricity prices through the strike threat. Nor is this pure grace-and-favour on their part. Union monopoly power is not a fixed, known quantity but something uncertain which can be increased by investing resources in organisation and strike funds.

In a highly unionised society some tacit conventions about acceptable relative wages have to be followed if Hobbesian anarchy is to be avoided. The rules of the game have never been spelt out. But what are felt to be legitimate relativities probably embody a mixture of market and historically determined differentials and traditional ideas of status (such as the

[1] R. Price and G. S. Bain, *Profiles of Union Growth*, Blackwell, Oxford, 1981.

relativities between the Archbishops of Canterbury and York). The quasi-moral element attaching to the result is an essential part of the enforcement mechanism. This situation is very different from the usual idea of a market equilibrium. I would prefer to call it a 'balance of forces', not exclusively economic. (There is no reason for an advocate of market forces to sign up for that union of economists which regards all mention of sociological factors as an act of intellectual blacklegging.)

The logic of the incomes policy case (rarely stated for fear of offending unions) is: (a) union power has added to the sustainable rate of unemployment by distorting the market pattern of real wages; and (b) incomes policy can reproduce something more nearly approaching market wages. I have explained elsewhere in some detail why proposition (b) is false.[1]

Unions have contributed to the trend rise in unemployment in most countries, not only through their direct industrial activities but, along with other producer lobbies, through their political influence. For instance, as a result of their insistence on Wages Councils which fix minimum wages, less-skilled people are priced out of work in low-pay industries. The union influence on the Manpower Services Commission (which has a tripartite board) ensures that it treads very gingerly with measures which will price young people *into* work. Policy concessions to union leaders have in practice been a feature of every post-war incomes policy in the UK. Nor can an incomes policy without such concessions be realistically conceived. Trade union leaders will not abandon their real or supposed control over wages, which is the basis of their prestige, except in return for some other gain.

Policy measures to reinforce union power in Britain have included state encouragement of the closed or union shop and the extension of union immunity from the normal processes of contract law. Concessions in return for promised wage restraint have also included controls on prices, profit margins and dividends, which merely discourage risk investment. Other examples are higher council house and mortgage subsidies and the tightening of rent control. Further, some phases of incomes policies have tried to squeeze pay differentials, both by differ-

---

[1] S. Brittan and P. Lilley, *The Delusion of Incomes Policy*, Temple Smith, 1977. This is updated in my chapter in R. E. J. Chater, A. Dean, R. F. Elliott (eds.), *Incomes Policies*, Oxford University Press (forthcoming).

ential pay norms and punitive taxation (i.e. purely political taxation which has no significant revenue yield).

The main effect of all these measures has been to inhibit the efficient functioning of the relevant markets (and thereby to aggravate, to take one example, the housing shortage). The reason why so many of them destroy productive jobs and create unemployment is that either they directly reduce the incentive to satisfy potential demand (price and rent controls) or they involve deliberately punitive taxation. The latter is either passed on, and therefore fails in its objective, or reduces the supply of key factors of production—whether skilled workers, top quality specialists, or managers of physical capital in risky ventures. Such people have tended to vote with their feet—by emigrating, moving into the black economy, or settling for a quiet life. Incomes policies have also sought to 'level up' the incomes of the lower-paid. While a laudable intention, the effect, like that of minimum wage laws in the United States, is to price out of work a large number of less-qualified workers.

Are these policies nevertheless worth buying as the price of persuading unions to accept some *average wage* figure nearer to market-clearing levels? Or is any gain more than offset by the myriad of particular and individual market distortions required to secure acquiescence? The common-sense answer is that, at a time of monetary squeeze, the impact of really tough and politically well-implemented pay policies may be favourable to employment; but after a while the favourable effect wears off and the distortions come to predominate.

To test conclusively the effect of incomes policies would require specific knowledge of how unemployment would have behaved without them, which we do not possess. But we can examine the movement of UK and international unemployment during the latest period when pay policies were in vogue. Over the six-year cycle to 1979, unemployment deteriorated in nearly all major countries; but the deterioration was biggest in the UK (Chart 9). The jump in the British unemployment rate was also much higher than Germany's, even though Germany had no truck with pay and price controls.

Politics and pay

Formal incomes policy has had disappointing results; and periods of restraint have always been followed by bursts of pay rises. But the crucial argument concerns the adverse side-effects in so many directions. Incomes policy perpetuates the medieval myth that there is a 'just price' for people's services, known to men of goodwill, which differs from that established in the market. The inevitable result is that everyone's 'just reward' adds up to more than the total available. Indeed, the more that people, whether farmers or teachers or dockers, come to look to the state to secure their reward, the more unmanageable the economy becomes. For it is in the nature of the political process to buy off each piece of trouble when it arrives, irrespective of whether the actions taken are coherent when taken together.

The real harm of pay policies, both 'hard' ones based on wage and price controls of the kind discussed and 'soft' ones formulated in national forums (i.e. dialogues among leaders of unions, industry and government), is to encourage the belief that each person must look to the political process for his well-being. This strengthens the interest-group pressures by which the citizen has to press his case under a politicised system. Thus, far from reducing conflict as their sponsors intend, the policies introduce political conflict into every nook and cranny of personal and business life.

With or without a formal incomes policy, the public sector will always present a special problem; and conflict will sometimes have to be faced. The great advantage of cash limit constraints (compared to pay norms) is that they reduce the political element in pay disputes and the traumatic nature of government defeats in particular disputes, as well as allowing account to be taken of differences in labour markets and union power with the minimum of fuss. When the publicity spotlight is turned on individual settlements—whether by Mr Heath on the miners in 1974 or by Mr Callaghan on Ford in the autumn of 1978—they acquire a key status they do not possess when an attitude of benign neglect prevails.

Unemployment palliatives

There may be some scope for palliatives, such as employment subsidies, so long as their true logic is apparent. The logic of a job subsidy is that, instead of unemployed people being expected to price themselves into jobs by working for lower pay, the employer is given a subsidy to achieve the same effect. But it is not a costless option; and it will work only if taxpayers

[115]

are prepared to accept lower real incomes to pay for the subsidies. It can *appear* costless only because of (a) the erroneous assumption that the unemployed will remain permanently out of work without subsidies, and (b) a failure to evaluate indirect costs.

Some economists are too prone to argue that when unemployment is high there is little resource cost in employment creation schemes. They overlook the fact that most projects will require supervision, materials, components and other services which may well be drawn from parts of the economy where resources are scarce. Moreover, the multiplier effect of increased consumption of the unemployed will raise demand across the whole economy and will not be particularly concentrated on products utilising the kinds of labour in most surplus.[1] The whole object of a special employment scheme is that it is over and above any general stimulus which can be safely given to spending power.

It would be socially desirable to grant employment subsidies to individuals with low earning capacity on a tapering basis so that there were no violent displacement effects slightly higher up the income scale. But, as a matter of administrative practice, they have to be given to companies, industries or public authorities. This constitutes a major difficulty.

Most existing special employment measures are of the job-subsidy character. The MSC estimated that nearly 360,000 jobs were attributable to such measures at the end of 1980, after taking into account employees who might have found work in any case, the substitution of eligible employees for other individuals no longer hired, and the displacement of other jobs elsewhere in the economy. Overwhelmingly, the two most important schemes were the Temporary Short-Time Working Compensation Scheme and the Youth Opportunities Programme.

The two principal additions proposed in the academic literature are (a) temporary recruitment subsidies for firms hiring members of the long-term unemployed, and (b) a subsidy for each net additional worker for firms expanding their

---

[1] Economists who believe that, so long as unemployment is below some target percentage, resources are free (not only in recessions but over a whole trade cycle and even in booms) will regard these costs as benefits. In pseudo-philosophical jargon, they are operating in a paradigm incompatible with this *Paper* and which it is trying to displace.

labour force.[1] The first idea is much the better of the two. Its main justification is that, with its aid, some of the long-term unemployed might rebuild their morale and skills and eventually be worth employing without the subsidy. Special payments for net additions to employment, on the other hand, will distort competition, encourage manipulation of corporate structure, and be unlikely to channel the benefits to those workers either most needing or deserving support from the rest of the country.

The fashionable advocacy of public *investment* is based on a misconception of even the basic Keynesian ideas which, if they are right, would point to additional spending of any kind, whether consumption or investment. Public sector *employment* schemes are a different matter. They can be financed by savings of social security benefits only if the wages of those taken into employment are less than the benefits they would otherwise receive grossed up for tax—plus some allowance for materials and administration. A scheme which really did meet these conditions would work by undercutting union wages and could be expected to run into the most vehement opposition from public sector unions.

The requirement that 'special employment schemes' should either pay for themselves or be financed by reductions in other public expenditure or by increased tax revenue is not a fundamental principle. It is a crude but essential check against wishful thinking. Without such a constraint the schemes will simply be a backdoor method of trying to spend our way to target levels of employment, with all the risks, discussed at length in this *Paper*, of accelerating inflation followed by an even more severe slump.

Indeed, when special employment measures take the form of permanent subsidies for loss-making industries—whether old-established ones, such as steel and cars, or high-technology ventures in aerospace—the result is worse than that of old-fashioned demand management. For then the result is not simply higher inflation but the forcible diversion of resources into activities which consumers at home and abroad have already voted against with their purses. A generalised increase in the budget deficit would be less harmful. Lame-duck subsidies could have a temporary rôle in deliberately slowing down the pace of industrial change to make human adjustment easier.

[1] Richard Layard, *op. cit.*

The case against them is that the temporary becomes permanent and the emergency said to justify their existence never comes to an end.

Radical reform

There are those who believe that, until the power of unions and other monopolistic bodies and lobbies to fix levels of remuneration far above market rates is removed, the minimum sustainable rate of unemployment will be disastrously high. This is the core of the Peter Jay catastrophe thesis.[1]

The political prize (which may be awarded in heaven rather than by the electorate) deserves to go to whichever leaders can help establish a better-functioning and more flexible labour market. There are only three radical models on offer. One is the Hayek approach which, although not spelt out in detail, is designed to deprive unions of their strike-threat powers. Another is the Jay proposal to abolish the wage relationship by transforming major enterprises into workers' co-operatives. Politically in-between is the Meade scheme to simulate the labour market by wage-fixing tribunals whose ultimate sanction would be the Hayekian withdrawal of legal privileges.[2]

The chances of any of these approaches being adopted are not bright. There is, however, a danger that some government waving the 'Meade' banner will drift back into crude wage- and price-fixing—which would be both a travesty of Professor Meade's own ideas and extremely unlikely to achieve the desired results.

The doom talk may be overdone. It is still possible that the present acute employment crisis represents a reaction to an uncertain inflationary environment and to a series of global shocks, all of which may pass. There would then be a case for an evolutionary piecemeal approach in which every change in union law, in housing policy, in capital market instruments or in state industrial aid would be judged by the criterion: 'Will it move wages and prices in the relevant markets nearer to or further from market-clearing levels?'.

[1] P. Jay, *Inflation, Unemployment and Politics*, Occasional Paper 46, IEA, 1976. Also his contribution to A. Clayre (ed.), *The Political Economy of Co-operation*, Blackwell, Oxford, 1980.

[2] The latest version is described in Professor Meade's chapter in David Lipsey and Dick Leonard (eds.), *The Socialist Agenda*, Cape, 1981.

At the moment, however, despite Mrs Thatcher, the institutionalised pricing of people out of work and the discouragement of occupational and geographical mobility in the name of better pensions and cheaper housing are still the mainsprings of government policy. There is an agenda a hundred miles long for the non-corporatists in a reformist party free from trade union strings and willing to judge arguments on their merits rather than by their labels.

VII. POLITICAL IMPLICATIONS AND CONCLUSIONS

If it is true, a doctrine which denies the ability of post-war demand management to achieve chosen levels of full employment is equally true for a Clause Four socialist, a social democrat, a Conservative 'wet' and a *laissez-faire* enthusiast. If untrue, it is untrue for all. The same applies to the relationship between the quantity of spending power and the price level.

To demonstrate how the issues discussed in this *Paper* cut across normal political allegiances, it is worth pointing out that the main pioneer among Chicago economists in the 1930s of the constant money supply growth rule was Paul Douglas, a Democrat who accepted nearly all the left-wing platform of his time—such as a 'planned economy', public housing and the encouragement of unions. Douglas became a war hero, a US Senator, and a hawk on Cold War issues; but he never abandoned his advocacy of interventionist and egalitarian domestic policies. He also continued to champion the monetarist rule, and was a moving force behind the Treasury-Federal Reserve Accord of 1951 which abandoned the pegging of interest rates and opened the way to Fed control of the money supply.

Although, today, purely political exponents of the counter-revolution tend to be on the right, economic exponents are scattered along the spectrum. They can and do disagree on income redistribution, government spending, or the rôle of union power in high unemployment. They would agree, however, that spending our way to target employment levels through monetary and fiscal expansion is not an option and, if followed, would lead to runaway inflation and yet more unemployment at some later date.

Cause-and-effect relationships are not themselves political. But it is only candid to point out that they can have political implications. If certain theories are true, some types of policy become impossible to pursue successfully—at least without making radical changes in the environment. There is nothing objective, impartial, academic or non-partisan in refusing to discuss such implications.

[120]

Marxists could legitimately point out that there is an uneasy resemblance between Friedman's 'natural rate of unemployment' (my CIR or MIR) and Marx's reserve army of the unemployed. Where the Marxists go wrong is in believing that the mere transfer of ownership could abolish this army without also removing valuable properties of the existing system, such as personal choice of job, consumer freedom to spend where he or she wishes, freedom to organise collectively, and an adequate social security minimum.

The response of many Keynesians to the intellectual crisis is to say that conventional demand management would still work if only it was combined with wage and price controls, or import controls, or state industrial intervention, or all these things together. It has thus become a totally different system to which Keynesians of the original variety need owe no allegiance whatever. Indeed, the counter-revolutionaries who want to tackle inflation from the demand side are closer to the original Keynesian spirit than those who use the label—even though they want to manage monetary rather than real demand and aim, as Keynes himself did in the 1920s, at stable or very gently rising prices rather than at specific employment objectives.

A strategy for full employment

A strategy for full employment in today's circumstances has to concentrate heavily on matters such as education, apprenticeship, regional policy, the work of official job placement centres, the detail of work contracts and pension arrangements, as well as temporary palliatives and many other matters which cannot be squeezed into the tail-end of a work on demand management. Such management can provide only a framework which would help avoid the worst instabilities. When the post of Chief Economic Adviser to the Government is located at the Department of Employment (which used to be called the Ministry of Labour and is the Department concerned directly with many of the matters discussed above), and when the best economic brains in the private sector are no longer employed in forecasting small movements in gilt-edged prices arising from the inconsistencies of monetary policy but are working in industry or the non-financial services sector, then we will know that the British economic miracle has arrived.

APPENDIX

The Lump of Labour Fallacy

Unemployment can never be zero in a free society, however well functioning. So long as people are allowed to spend time between jobs and not forced to accept the first available offer, some will be out of work. Their number will be increased by mismatches in demand and supply in terms of skills or geographical location. Provided some financial support is available to the unemployed, whether from the dole, family and friends or savings, wages will not plunge or soar to clear every labour market—even in the absence of unions, minimum wage laws or other institutional obstacles. Moreover, it is neither humane nor economically desirable that every market should clear instantly.

The final part of this *Paper* discussed the forces which make the margin of unutilised labour unduly high, causing unnecessary hardship and social waste. But popular discussion goes far beyond the idea of a margin, desirable or otherwise. It is governed by the belief that there is a limited amount of work to be done and that society is threatened by a chronic and increasing shortage of jobs as technology advances. This is known as the 'lump of labour fallacy'. It is typified by remarks such as: 'Once we bring all this overmanning to an end, there just won't be the jobs to go round'. It is a maddening fallacy because, if believed and acted upon, it could halt all improvement and impoverish us all quite needlessly.

The 'fixed amount of production fallacy' might be a more accurate name for it. For it presupposes there is a fixed amount of goods and services to be produced and that, if anything happens to enable that work to be done with fewer hands or to increase the supply of labour, the result must be more unemployment or compulsory work-sharing. The fallacy rears its head when trade unions call for a shorter working week to combat unemployment, or when so-called experts look with alarm at the likely growth of the European labour force, wondering 'where the jobs to employ it will come from'. If it were true, the man who 'could make two ears of corn or two blades of grass' grow where one grew before, far from being worth 'more than the whole race of politicians put together', would be the enemy of mankind.

The same kind of attitude underlies the recent concern about the micro-chip computer, the desire to reduce retiring ages or push young people into more years of full-time education, and much other nonsense. Alarm has been expressed whenever an apparently labour-saving invention has appeared. Few people now remember the scare when the earliest types of automation appeared in the motor industry in the 1950s; but other examples go back much further—well beyond the Luddites who roamed the country after the Napoleonic Wars destroying machinery. In the 16th century sheep were believed to be 'eating up' jobs on the land. No doubt the same charge was levelled at the inventors of the plough and the wheel.

Unfortunately, no amount of technical or professional training is proof against this type of thinking in the absence of a feeling for the outrageous absurdity of certain propositions. Indeed, some of the worst offenders are people whose expertise in statistical projection and flair for flesh-creeping headlines exceed their economic common-sense.

Doom-watch forecasts

Many doom-watch unemployment forecasts are based on little more than a projection of the rise in population of working age plus a high trend in productivity attributed to the micro-chip or other fashionable invention. Suppose the addition of the two suggests that output will need to grow in the future at an annual rate of 5 per cent (a figure more characteristic of some Continental countries than of the UK) compared with a growth trend in the recent past of 3 per cent. Projecting the two rates generates an ever-increasing 'employment gap' of 2 per cent a year compound until ultimately everybody is out of a job.

Innovations which raise productivity at given wage levels normally reduce costs and prices and thus enlarge spending power. It happens to be true that the most rapid increases in employment have taken place in industries like electronics where productivity has risen most quickly. But even if the facts were to change and large productivity improvements were to occur in industries such as salt production or bread-baking where price is not very responsive to demand and there is little long-term growth, the point about releasing purchasing power would still apply. If the government is committed to stabilising Money GNP, as urged in this *Paper*, that will provide a fail-safe device against any temporary failure of people's imagination in finding new ways of spending higher incomes.

The worst outcome for employment would be in the event of insufficient capital or entrepreneurial skill to employ workers displaced by technological progress. This can be the case even when published surveys show excess capacity, if much of it is obsolete, although its owners may not know it. Such results can occur, for

[123]

instance, after a de-manning drive.[1] Even then the availability of labour will itself encourage investment to make use of it, provided savings are adequate (not a problem at present) and provided workers—or those who act on their behalf—are willing to price themselves into jobs (which is much more of a difficulty).

Calculations of an ineradicable 'employment gap' are an example of the 'economics without price' which clouds so much thinking. Such calculations take no account either of the probability of growth (counting *voluntary* leisure as a form of growth) speeding up to take advantage of a bigger supply of labour; or of the effects of a surplus of workers in reducing the rewards of labour relatively to that of capital, and thus promoting the use of more labour-intensive methods. None of this means that adjustment will work well. My criticism is that silly arithmetic is substituted for the analysis of labour markets and that misguided people pay their own and tax-payers' money for such studies.

Economic satiation 'a long way off'

The fallacy is sometimes expressed in terms of the satiation of human wants. The sign that satiation had arrived would be that there was nothing on which people wished to spend extra incomes. Until you observe people being indifferent to increases in real pay, or seeking them exclusively to pile up savings which they neither intend to spend later nor bequeath or donate to others who will spend, you may be sure that satiation has not arrived.

If it did arrive, we would be in a state not of depression but of economic bliss. Technical progress would then be enjoyed by workers in the form of reduced working hours without loss of take-home pay; and this would happen quite voluntarily through normal bargaining. Thus it would not be unemployment in the sense of enforced idleness.

If satiation was really here, few would be interested in winning the football pools; and people might well continue to work in their chosen occupations regardless of reward. We are a very long way from such a state of affairs. Satiation of wants—even in Western industrialised countries, let alone in the poor Third World—does not pass muster as an explanation of present-day unemployment.

---

[1] Technical progress which reduces the share of labour in national income in relation to that of capital is said in some textbooks to be 'labour-saving and capital-using'. This does not mean merely that the same output can be produced with fewer workers, which is a characteristic of most technical progress. It means that technical progress is slower in the capital goods sector than in the rest of the economy, so that capital becomes scarcer and its return rises relatively to labour. The textbook definition is that the marginal product of capital rises more than proportionately to that of labour. (For instance, Harry Johnson, *The Theory of Distribution*, Gray-Mills Publishing, London, 1973.)

The various work-sharing gimmicks such as reduced hours or early retirement might, if earnings per hour were not raised, increase the demand for labour. But, if the demand for labour is already as high as is consistent with a non-accelerating rate of inflation, any further increase will be temporary and self-defeating. If, on the other hand, it is safe to increase the demand for labour, why not do so directly by expansionary monetary and fiscal policies rather than by wasteful work-sharing methods?

Above all—and this is where we come to the present-day practical point—work-sharing would not resolve the problems of labour market frictions, monopolistic wage setting and union wage push which make it impossible to have full employment. Indeed, if the working week was reduced to 20 hours for everyone next year, there might well be no reduction in unemployment—and possibly even an increase.

TOPICS FOR DISCUSSION

1. 'The error of most post-war demand management was to assume that real things, such as output and employment, could invariably and as a matter of course be affected permanently by financial manipulation'. Discuss.

2. Explain and evaluate the author's contention that focussing on Money GDP as the ultimate target of financial policy 'provides a bridge between the more reasonable Friedman-ites and the more reasonable Keynesians'.

3. 'A successful regime of monetary targets provides a powerful check on fiscal behaviour'. Explain.

4. What are the arguments for and against macro-economic policy being guided by targets for, respectively, the following factors: (a) employment, (b) output, (c) prices, (d) money supply, (e) budget surplus/deficit, (f) Money GDP?

5. Do you find the concept of the minimum sustainable rate of unemployment a useful analytical tool? What is the most effective way to discover how high it is in a given economy?

6. Explain and evaluate the theory of the 'constant employment budget'.

7. Describe the principal factors which determine the demand for and supply of labour.

8. What are the major drawbacks of formal incomes policies?

9. How do badly-functioning markets for labour, capital, housing and other resources raise unemployment?

10. Explain and evaluate the 'lump of labour fallacy'.

SELECT BIBLIOGRAPHY

The reader's problem will not be to find additional reading material but to escape drowning in a sea of it. There are probably tens of thousands of books and articles relevant to this essay — far too many. Each publication itself contains references to scores of others.

The following list is confined to a few publications which bear most directly on the issues raised by this *Paper* or which enlarge on matters to which I have alluded briefly.

Ball, J., *Money and Employment*, Macmillan, London, 1981 (forthcoming).

——, and Burns, T., 'The Inflationary Mechanism in the UK Economy', *American Economic Review*, No. 66, 1976.

——, Burns, T., and Laury, J., 'The Role of Exchange Rate Changes in the Balance of Payments Adjustment', *Economic Journal*, March 1977.

Beenstock, Michael, 'The Debate about Monetary Ceilings', *Economic Outlook, 1980-84*, London Business School, Gower Publishing, Vol. 5, No. 1, October 1980.

——, and Willcocks, Patrick, *The Consequences of Slower Growth in the World Economy*, Economic Forecasting Unit Discussion Paper 76, London Business School, 1980.

Budd, Alan, 'Recent Developments in Monetarism', *British Review of Economic Issues*, Vol. 2, No. 7, November 1980.

——, and Burns, T., 'Why the Exchange Rate Must be Set Free', *Economic Outlook*, London Business School, April 1977.

Bresciana-Turroni, C., *The Economics of Inflation*, 1931; English edn., Augustus Kelly, New York, 1937, reprinted 1968.

Brittan, Samuel, *Second Thoughts on Full Employment Policy*, Barry Rose for the Centre for Policy Studies, 1975.

——, *The Economic Consequences of Democracy*, Temple Smith, London, 1977.

——, and Lilley, P., *The Delusion of Incomes Policy*, Temple Smith, London, 1977.

Caves, R. E. and Krause, L. B. (eds.), *Britain's Economic Performance*, The Brookings Institution, Washington DC, 1980.

Cipolla, C. M., *Money, Prices and Civilisation in the Mediterranean World*, Princeton University Press, 1956.

Clayre, Alasdair (ed.), *The Political Economy of Co-operation and Participation*, Oxford University Press, 1979.

Report of the Committee to Review the Functioning of Financial Institutions ('Wilson Committee'), Cmnd. 7937, HMSO, 1980.

Congdon, Tim, 'The First Principles of Central Banking', *The Banker*, April 1981.

Laidler, David, Tobin, James, *et al.*, 'Symposium on Monetarism', *Economic Journal*, March 1981.

Eltis, W. A., and Sinclair, P. J. N., 'Money Supply and Exchange Rate', *Oxford Economic Papers*, July 1981, and Oxford University Press, 1981.

Fisher, Irving, 'A Statistical Relation Between Unemployment and Price Changes', *International Labour Review*, June 1926.

Friedman, Milton, *The Optimum Quantity of Money*, University of Chicago Press, 1969.

——, *Essays in Positive Economics*, University of Chicago Press, 1953.

——, 'Inflation and Unemployment' (1976 Alfred Nobel Memorial Lecture), *Journal of Political Economy*, 1977. Also Occasional Paper 51, Institute of Economic Affairs, 1977.

——, *The Counter-Revolution in Monetary Theory*, Occasional Paper 33, Institute of Economic Affairs, 1970.

——, 'A Theoretical Framework for Monetary Analysis', *Journal of Political Economy*, Vol. 78, No. 2, 1970.

——, and Schwartz, Anna, *A Monetary History of the United States*, Princeton University Press, 1963.

Field, Frank, *Inequality in Britain*, Fontana, 1981.

Flemming, John, *Inflation*, Oxford University Press, 1976.

Forsyth, P. J., and Kay, J. A., 'The Economic Implications of North Sea Oil', *Fiscal Studies*, July 1980.

Free Life, 'Monetarism' Special Issue Vol. 1, No. 4, Autumn 1980 (Libertarian Alliance, 40 Floral Street, London, W.C.2).

Hayek, F. A., *Denationalisation of Money—The Argument Refined*, Hobart Paper 70, 2nd edn., Institute of Economic Affairs, 1978.

——, *1980s Unemployment and the Unions*, Hobart Paper 87, Institute of Economic Affairs, 1980.

Howell, Ralph, *Why Work?*, Conservative Political Centre, 2nd edn., 1981.

Hume, David, *Enquiries*, ed. L. A. Selby-Bigge, Oxford University Press, 1902, reprinted 1966.

Jay, Peter, *Inflation, Unemployment and Politics*, Occasional Paper 46, Institute of Economic Affairs, 1976.

Johnson, H. G., *Economics and Society*, University of Chicago Press, 1975.

Keynes, J. M., *The General Theory of Employment, Interest and Money*, Macmillan, 1st edition, 1936, new edition, 1973.

Laidler, D., *Essays on Money and Inflation*, Manchester University Press, 1975.

Minford, P., and associates, 'Is the Government's Strategy on Course?', *Lloyds Bank Review*, 1981, and Liverpool Occasional Papers No. 1, 1981.

Layard, R., Metcalf, D., and Nickell, S., *The Effect of Collective Bargaining on Wages*, London School of Economics, Mimeo, 1977.

——, *Unemployment in Britain: Causes and Cures*, Centre for Labour Economics, London School of Economics, 1981.

Leonard, Dick, and Lipsey, David (eds.), *The Socialist Agenda*, Cape, 1981.

Nickell, S. J., 'The Effect of Unemployment and Related Benefits on the Duration of Unemployment', *Economic Journal*, March 1979.

Niehans, Jürg, *The Theory of Money*, Johns Hopkins University Press, 1978.

——, *The Appreciation of Sterling*, Centre for Policy Studies, 1981.

Pencavel, J. H., 'The Distributional and Efficiency Aspects of Trade Unionism in Britain', *British Journal of Industrial Relations*, 1977.

Phillips, A. W., 'The Relationship between Unemployment and the Rate of Change of Money Wages in the UK, 1861-1957', *Economica*, 1958, pp. 783-791; reprinted in *Inflation* (ed. Ball and Doyle), Penguin, 1969.

Rueff, J., 'Les Variations du Chômage en Angleterre', *Revue Politique et Parlementaire*, Paris, 1925.

Symons, J., *The Demand for Labour in British Manufacturing*, Centre for Labour Economics, London School of Economics, 1981.

Walters, A. A., *Money in Boom and Slump*, Hobart Paper 44, 3rd edn., Institute of Economic Affairs, 1971.

Centre for Labour Economics, London School of Economics, *Discussion Papers*, 1978 *et seq.*

Economica, Issue on Unemployment, August 1980.

Financial Statement and Budget Report ('Red Book'), especially for 1980-81 and 1981-82, HMSO.

Organisation for Economic Co-Operation and Development (OECD), *Towards Full Employment and Price Stability* (McCracken Report), HMSO, 1977.

OECD, *Economic Outlook,* July and December, 1980, HMSO, 1981.

Treasury and Civil Service Committee, *Monetary Policy Report* and Volumes of Evidence, 1980, House of Commons, HMSO, 1981.

US Council of Economic Advisers, *Report to the President*, US Government Printing Office, Washington, DC 20402, 1981.

Some recent IEA Papers on Monetary Policy

Hobart Paper 88
Monopoly in Money and Inflation
The Case for a Constitution to Discipline Government
H. GEOFFREY BRENNAN and JAMES M. BUCHANAN
1981 £1.50

'The professors contend that history has shown that governments, far from being benevolent, have been "malevolent despots".'
Guardian

Readings 24
Is Monetarism Enough?
Essays in refining and reinforcing the monetary cure for inflation
PATRICK MINFORD, HAROLD ROSE, WALTER ELTIS,
MORRIS PERLMAN, JOHN BURTON
1980 £3.00

'The reader of this book may not come away with any easy answers, but he will be made aware of the issues currently under discussion in the monetarist debate and of the difficulties of making monetarism a workable policy.'
Banker

Occasional Paper 44
Unemployment *versus* Inflation?
An evaluation of the Phillips Curve
MILTON FRIEDMAN
with a British Commentary by David Laidler
1975 4th Impression 1981 £1.00

'. . . a standard piece of reading for all future Chancellors.'
Daily Express

'. . . what is perhaps the most important economic pamphlet to be published in the UK for several decades.'
Samuel Brittan, *Financial Times*

Occasional Paper 51
Inflation and Unemployment: The New Dimension of Politics
MILTON FRIEDMAN
1977 2nd Impression 1978 £1.50

'I have to warn you that there is neither shock nor horror nor sensation in his lecture, only close reasoning, and a sense of scholarly inquiry . . . I urge readers to buy and read [it].'
Patrick Hutber, *Sunday Telegraph*

[131]

[132]